THE
UNIVERSITY
OF MICHIGAN
IN **CHINA**

The University of Michigan

in CHINA

DAVID WARD AND EUGENE CHEN

MAIZE BOOKS

Copyright © 2017 by the Regents of the University of Michigan
All rights reserved

This book may not be reproduced, in whole or in part, including illustrations, in any form (beyond that copying permitted by Sections 107 and 108 of the US Copyright Law and except by reviewers for the public press), without written permission from the publisher.

Published in the United States of America by
Michigan Publishing
Manufactured in the United States of America

DOI: http://dx.doi.org/10.3998/mpub.9885197

ISBN 978-1-60785-427-2 (paper)
ISBN 978-1-60785-428-9 (e-book)

An imprint of Michigan Publishing, Maize Books serves the publishing needs of the University of Michigan community by making high-quality scholarship widely available in print and online. It represents a new model for authors seeking to share their work within and beyond the academy, offering streamlined selection, production, and distribution processes. Maize Books is intended as a complement to more formal modes of publication in a wide range of disciplinary areas.

http://www.maizebooks.org

CONTENTS

Foreword	vii
Preface	ix
Acknowledgments	xiii
1. Introduction	1
2. The 19th Century: The University Reaches Out to China	4
The Tenure and Diplomacy of James Burrill Angell	9
Angell's Legacy	16
3. Kang Cheng and Shi Meiyu: The University of Michigan's First Chinese Students	20
A Michigan Missionary Alone in China	21
Education between Two Cultures: Late 19th Century	23
Putting Down Roots at the End of the Qing Dynasty	26
Diverging Paths: Shi Meiyu and Conflict with the Missionary Society	29
Kang Cheng: An Accidental Diplomat at the Birth of a New China	33
A Legacy of Selflessness	37
4. The Barbour Scholars	38
Ding Maoying: Hospital Director, Aid Worker, and National Representative	41
Wu Yifang: China's First Female College President	51
Barbour's Legacy	60

5. Turn-of-the-Century Intellectuals   62
   Zheng Zuoxin: Father of Ornithology in China   64
   Wu Dayou: Father of Chinese Physics   66
   John C. H. Wu: Legal Scholar, Theologian, and
      Architect of the Republic of China's Constitution   72

6. Heroes and Survivors of World War II   82
   He Yizhen: "Studying to Save the Country"   84
   Robert Ellsworth Brown: Hero of the Nanjing Massacre   87
   Harmon of Michigan: Football Star, Fighter Pilot   93

7. Postwar Scientists in the People's Republic of China   102
   Wang Chengshu and Zhu Guangya: Pioneers of
      China's Nuclear Age   103
   Huang Jiasi: At the Helm of Surgery in New China   113
   Zeng Chengkui: Father of Marine Botany   117

8. The University of Michigan and Ping-Pong Diplomacy   128
   Ping-Pong Takes Center Stage   130
   Alexander Eckstein, the University of Michigan,
      and the Open Door of Diplomacy   133

9. The University of Michigan and China   140
   Education Expands   141
   Cultural Exchange at the University of Michigan   144
   Toward the Future   148

FOREWORD

The University of Michigan (U-M) is known throughout the world as a leading international community of scholars. U-M has admitted international students since the late 1840s, and our first foreign-born faculty member was hired in 1846. Throughout our 200-year history, we have been strengthened by pioneering individuals from around the world whose achievements have helped shape our legacy as a great public research university.

Our relationship with China is an essential component of our heritage. When the University's third president, James B. Angell, took leave in 1880 to serve as the US minister to China, he forged a connection that exists to this day. The University of Michigan continues to excel as a home to top scholars, influential projects, and exciting research through multiple international academic partnerships, robust exchanges of students, and leading academic collaborations such as our Kenneth G. Lieberthal and Richard H. Rogel Center for Chinese Studies.

The University of Michigan in China shares the stories of those who have helped create one of the most productive international collaborations in all of higher education. The book chronicles some of the most pivotal events in the history of two nations and profiles visionary leaders who saw the enormous potential of a relationship that could nurture scholars and students from two different hemispheres.

The University of Michigan's ability to attract the best students and faculty from around the globe enhances everything we do. Our teaching, research, patient care, and societal impact are all made better when we can leverage the perspectives and experiences of as many diverse individuals as possible.

When students and faculty come here from other countries, and when our students and faculty go elsewhere around the world, everyone involved benefits. They experience different cultures and discover the common aspirations of all humankind. The better we know and understand people from other parts of the globe, the less likely our international disagreements are to spin into dangerous conflicts.

I am deeply honored to lead a university that has such a long and distinguished history of close relations with China. My first international trip as president of the University was to China, and it was a pleasure to meet with the researchers, students, and alumni who are building on our legacy of collaboration.

I look forward to further strengthening our wonderful partnerships with China's universities, students, and institutions. Bolstered by nearly two centuries of mutual success, I believe the University of Michigan and China are poised to advance prosperity and understanding among the people of our nations.

Mark Schlissel
President

PREFACE

The adventuresome, often courageous lives of the University of Michigan (U-M) students, teachers, and leaders in this book emerge marked by the historical dramas of their times, Chinese and American. But the motivating power that kept them on a steady course was almost always a desire to help their country, sometimes Christian teachings, and also a passion for education. While this movement from the University to build relations in China was getting started, there was another movement in the other direction, from China to the Western world. Some missionaries and diplomats brought Chinese culture back to the English-speaking world. An example is the Scottish missionary, sinologist, and translator of the Chinese philosophical classics James Legge (1815–1897). When I assumed my position as an assistant professor of Chinese philosophy at the University in 1964, I had students in my undergraduate courses consult some of Legge's works. By this time, the University of Michigan Center for Chinese Studies was just getting under way and other China connections were being developed outside the University.

In the case of the earliest Chinese students, they were often aided by either a missionary from the United States or the generosity of someone at Michigan. Their graduate specialties were often in fields minimally present in China: medicine, physics, biological sciences, and international law. Two young female Chinese, Kang Cheng and Shi Meiyu, were adopted by a China-based missionary from Ypsilanti. They entered the University of Michigan Medical School in 1892.

Among the historical events at this time was the pressure in the United States to prohibit Chinese immigration. But the University's longest-serving president, James B. Angell (38 years) was at the helm at the moment in which there was both a treaty awarding China the status of "most favored nation" and also increased pressure to block Chinese immigration, especially of laborers. In 1880, the secretary of state asked Angell to go to China as a minister to revise the United States' China treaties. There were cocommissioners in the delegation. One favored a total ban on Chinese. Angell favored an open door, and that stance prevailed when he returned in 1882. But then US president Chester A. Arthur signed the Chinese Exclusion Act, which barred both skilled and unskilled laborers from entering the United States. That barrier facing Kang and Shi was surmounted with the political help of the Methodist Church and the influence of President Angell. The two women graduated with distinction, wearing Chinese garments at the ceremony. The act was not rescinded until World War II.

Back in China in 1900, the Boxer Rebellion of peasants, aimed at driving foreigners from China, had imperial backing. Once the rebellion was broken, with military support from Europe and Japan, China was required to pay indemnities to those powers. President Angell helped the US authorities channel their share of the money back into scholarships in the United States for Chinese students. Meanwhile, our two graduates, Kang and Shi, had set up a clinic at the Women's Foreign Missionary Society in Jiangxi province, motivated by both Christian values and the nationalist sentiment to "save China through education." They were paid less than the other staff and could not live in the missionary compound. Eventually they set up an independent clinic in Shanghai. After the successful anti-Manchu rebellion of 1911, China entered a period of fracture under various warlords. That meant more danger for the doctors Kang and Shi, excitingly described in this book. Among the legacies from Shi Meiyu was a modern nursing education system, established in Jiujiang, Jiangxi province, that aimed to lower the high infant mortality rate.

Since its founding in 1914 by Michigan graduate and regent Levi Barbour, 700 Asian women (among other nationalities: Indian, Chinese, Turkish) have received undergraduate scholarships or graduate fellowships. Many said that they not only are grateful for that opportunity but also have positive memories of their lives in Ann Arbor. One wrote that, immersed in her hospital work after graduation, she longed for "a good walk in the woods" back at the Michigan campus. The Nichols Arboretum has had that impact on many graduates. The Michigan Law School graduate (class of 1921) John C. H. Wu helped write the Republic of China's constitution, translated the Daoist classic the *Daodejing*, and was a specialist in both traditional Chinese law and modern international law. He wrote that "my stay in Ann Arbor was among the happiest periods of my life." I remember being on the Michigan campus in 1973 when the Chinese ping-pong team arrived and the warm welcome with which the Michigan students greeted the Chinese visitors.

During World War II, Robert E. Brown, U-M MD and MPH, treated malaria affecting workers on the Burma Road. Not discussed in detail in this book are Richard Edwards (later a professor of Chinese art) and Rhoads Murphey (later a professor of Asian history), who drove the charcoal-fired ambulances and freight trucks in Yunnan province at the eastern end of the road.

The fate of Michigan graduates in China again had to flow with the current of the Maoist years. Back home, 1937 U-M physics PhD He Yizhen founded the Institute of Metal Research at the Beijing Chinese Academy of Sciences. During the 1966–1976 period, Mao instigated a violent attempt to refocus the Chinese Communist Party leaders away from a so-called capitalist economy emphasizing expertise and profit maximization and back toward the revolutionary spirit of the guerilla days. He called it the Cultural Revolution and closed all schools and universities, some for 10 years. Students and teachers were sent to the rural areas or deserts to do work with peasants. He Yizhen left the Academy of Sciences and did forced labor. Once Mao started China's nuclear weapons program, the 1941 Barbour Fellow Wang Chengshu was posted to a nuclear research station in the Gobi Desert, where the isolation protected her from the fate of Dr. He. One Michigan-trained ornithologist spent those years living in a cowshed.

As the relationship between the United States and China warmed in 1972, Michigan professor Alexander Eckstein and the nongovernmental organization he helped found, the National Committee on US-China Relations, took a step on the road to rapprochement with the instigation of ping-pong diplomacy. One morning in April 1973, I watched as the cheerful underdog American team played the stars from China in the top-floor ballroom of the Michigan Union.

On a personal level, I will conclude with remarks that reveal the breadth of the University's reception of Chinese students. After Mao's death, his successor, Deng Xiaoping, was still wary about the dilution of "Communist purity." A democracy movement in Tiananmen Square in 1989 led to an episode of military repression, in which many students and others were killed. The Communist Party claimed the movement was led by two or three persons, the "Black Hands of Beijing." Among them was the social scientist Chen Ziming. These so-called instigators were given long prison sentences. One of my own small roles in fostering the education of Chinese students at the University of Michigan began then. I had a request from Chen Ziming to study with me by mail and by phone while he was in prison. After a lengthy negotiation with the dean of the graduate school, John D'Arms, and others, I received permission to accept Chen's request. Allowing no publicity, I proceeded to line up two other U-M faculty members, and we all entered the teacher-student relationship with Chen Ziming. Using a quiet route to send him the books and printed material, I made sure he did the homework and took the exams. One such route was Leonard Woodcock. America's first ambassador to China (appointed in 1979) in the post–World War II era, while he lived in Ann Arbor, Woodcock became one of those who aided in the physical transmission of materials for Chen's studies. And Chen Ziming fulfilled his obligations. Twice he was released from prison on medical parole between 1994 and 1996. He continued his course work at home under house arrest, only to be imprisoned again for political activity. Released in 2002 on completion of his full term, he died of pancreatic cancer in 2014.

Chen's degree became a cross-continental relay, a feat of institutional and individual tenacity in the face of political opposition. The desire for education often succeeds in curious ways.

Donald J. Munro
Professor Emeritus of Philosophy and Chinese
April 7, 2017

ACKNOWLEDGMENTS

This book is a product of support from all corners of the University, the country, and (in fact) the world. It wouldn't exist at all without the backing of people like Dr. Liming Li, Drs. Joseph Kolars and Shaomeng Wang of the University of Michigan (U-M) Medical School, Brodie Remington of Michigan development, Dr. James Holloway in the office of the provost, and Dr. Jack Hu, the vice president for research at U-M.

The research process for this book relied on the generosity and good graces of many: the patient archivists at the Bentley Historical Library here at U-M; the General Commission on Archives and History at the United Methodist Church; the archives of the Harvard Law School, University of California at San Diego, State University of New York at Buffalo, the American Ornithological Society, the Gerald R. Ford Presidential Library, and Mount Holyoke College; Donna Albino and her private collection; and the Chinese University Press of Hong Kong and the People's Publishing House.

And finally, we owe a debt of gratitude to the collective enthusiasm of a whole bouquet of people: the University of Michigan Association of Chinese Professors; Anne Gere, director of the Sweetland Center for Writing; Kelly Espinoza; Amy Huang; the family of Harry Bouchard; Don Munro, for the conversation and contributions; and Joe and Julie, for reading and rereading chapters.

The University of Michigan in China

1 Introduction

The story of the University of Michigan (U-M) is the story of a university growing beyond state and national borders, of a university leading the American public in reaching out to other nations. Nowhere is this more visible than with China. The relationship between U-M and China reaches back more than a century and a half to the first years of the Ann Arbor campus and the last years of the Qing dynasty.

It was an era of contention between the East and the West: in China, the violence of the Opium Wars and the political exploitation that followed led to a mistrust of foreigners with imperialist inclinations; in America, economic hardship following the Civil War led to an increasing resentment of Chinese immigrants. The University of Michigan forged an alliance with China that ran counter to public sentiment on both sides. From Judson Collins, a member of U-M's first graduating class, who became a missionary in the city of Fuzhou, to James Angell, U-M's longest-serving president, who became a diplomat in Beijing and a voice of reason in the contentious immigration debate, to Kang Cheng and Shi Meiyu, U-M's first Chinese students, the latter half of the 19th century saw U-M initiate a partnership with China that replaced tension and distrust with education and good works.

The start of the 20th century followed through on this partnership. Encouraged by Angell, the return of the Boxer indemnity in the form of a scholarship fund for Chinese students studying in America meant that the number of Chinese students at the University of Michigan rose dramatically. And the Barbour Scholarship, endowed in 1917 by U-M regent Levi Barbour, meant that Chinese women had a new, crucial avenue to higher education. Graduates like Ding Maoying, John C. H. Wu, and Wu Dayou exemplify the importance of education at U-M during these years. Ding Maoying leapt straight from her medical degree to a position at the head of a hospital in

Tianjin; John C. H. Wu, building on the foundation of his U-M law degree, drafted the Republic of China's constitution; and Wu Dayou shaped the study of physics in both China and Taiwan.

The University of Michigan was with China during the war years. American graduates Robert Brown and Tom Harmon served in China as a doctor and an air force pilot supporting the Flying Tigers, respectively. Wu Yifang, a Barbour Scholar, became China's first female college president just in time to shepherd Jinling (Ginling) College through some of China's most difficult years. And although relations between the United States and China cooled with the Korean War, graduates from the University of Michigan played crucial roles in establishing the new People's Republic of China (PRC). Zhu Guangya helped orchestrate the PRC's burgeoning nuclear weapons program; Zeng Chengkui jump-started the discipline of marine botany, and his techniques for farming algae fed many people as famine loomed; and Huang Jiasi rose to the top of the leadership in the PRC's new medical institutions.

When it came time for rapprochement between the two countries, the University of Michigan was there, hosting the Chinese table tennis team and organizing the "return volley" of the ping-pong diplomacy that thawed relations between the People's Republic and the United States.

Now in the early years of the 21st century, the University of Michigan and China are old friends. There are more students from China at U-M than from any other foreign country. In departments all over the University, scholarship and travel programs, research collaborations, joint degree programs, and joint institutes spring up left and right. As it has ever been, U-M is not beholden to political trends or public sentiments. The benefits of friendship and the fruits of collaboration are too clear.

The story of the University of Michigan's friendship with China is the story of astonishing individuals. There are many "firsts" in this book—first female college president, first woman with a PhD in physics—and there are many "fathers" of disciplines. While much has been written separately about these leaders and scholars, in both English and Chinese, nowhere is their collective story told or their shared bond with U-M celebrated. It is the aim of this book, as a gift from the U-M Association of Chinese Professors, to celebrate this almost 200-year-old legacy.

Such is the wealth of China's contribution to the University of Michigan and the University's contributions to China that this book can only contain the smallest fragment of the stories worth telling. There are hundreds of Barbour Scholars not included in this book. There are whole schools at U-M whose history with China is yet untouched. The Ford School of Public Policy, for example, benefited from an influx of Chinese students in the early years of the 20th century, including Chen Yeyi, who became China's only female general during the Sino-Japanese War. And there are just as many American students and faculty who spent time in China during these years, such as Harry Bouchard, a civil engineer who taught in Tianjin.

There have been an extraordinary number of Chinese graduates from the University of Michigan in the last four decades. Their stories, and the story of U-M's continuing relationship with China, will—we hope—be told in future books. There is enough here to fill volumes.

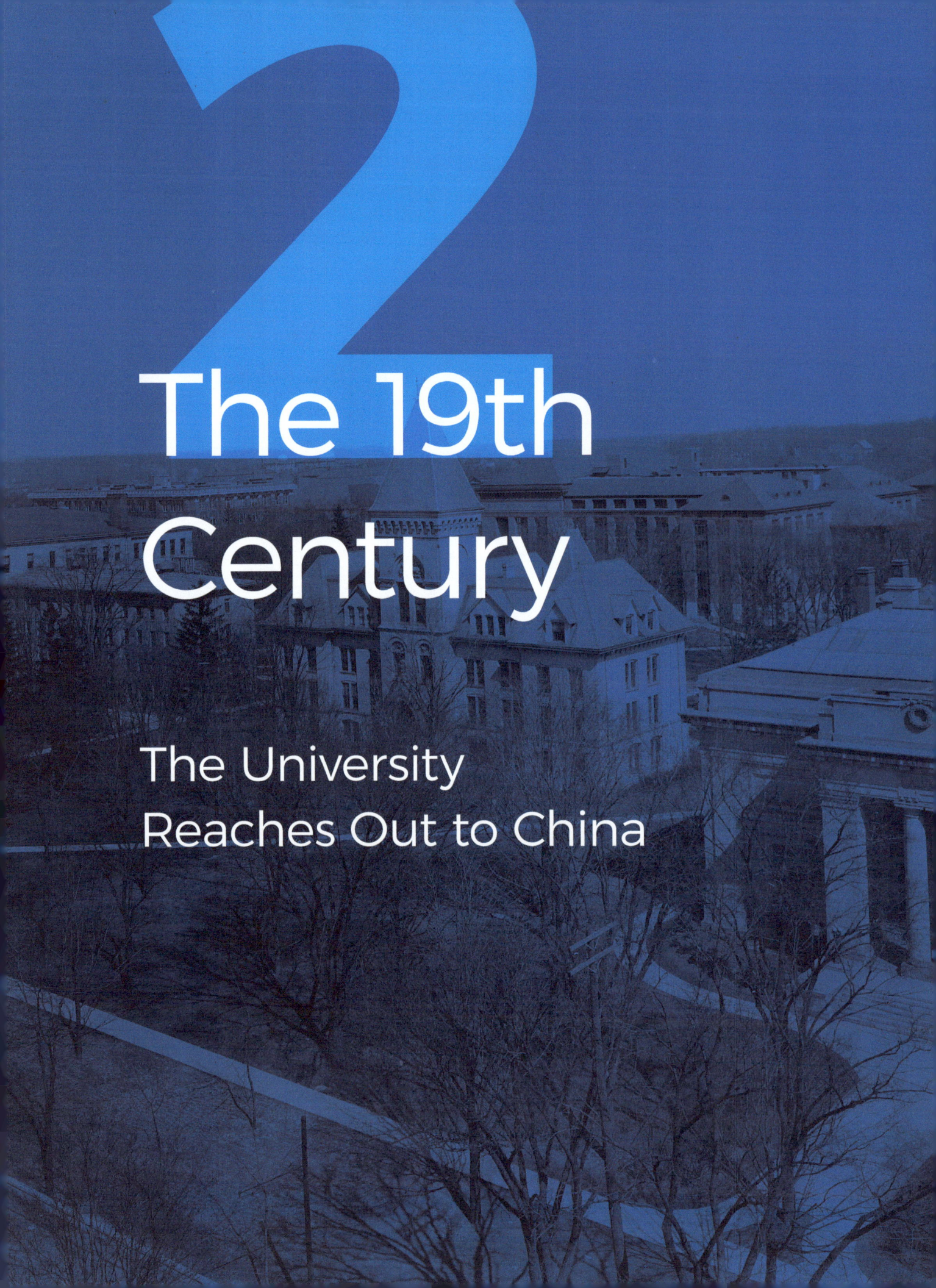

2

The 19th Century

The University Reaches Out to China

The University of Michigan's (U-M's) connection to China is almost as old as the University itself. In the school's early years, this relationship was shaped by American graduates who traveled to China as missionaries or naturalists. But the most prominent and politically important connection came with U-M president James Angell, whose service as a diplomat and minister in China paved the way for more than a century of close rapport between the institution and the nation.

In the autumn of 1841, when the First Opium War between the United Kingdom and the Qing dynasty was still a year away from its conclusion, the University of Michigan in Ann Arbor opened its doors for the first classes at the collegiate level. Six college students had enrolled in the Ann Arbor campus, then housed in one main building. Life in those early days was austere: students rose early, "awakened at 5 a.m. by a clanging bell" to attend a compulsory chapel devotion. They paid $1.50 per term for firewood, which they split themselves in the woodyard nearby and hauled, along with washing water, up to their rooms. Each living room "contained a study table, two chairs, a stove, and a wood closet" (Peckham 22). Students cleaned their own rooms, sweeping dirt and ashes from the stove out into the hall to be collected by the janitor, whom they nicknamed the "Professor of Dust and Ashes." As attendance grew, so too did the complexity of student life on campus. Despite the spartan living conditions and religious influence (attendance at a town church service was mandatory on Sundays, in addition to the daily chapel services), students organized "literary societies" and played pranks on the faculty and each other, building bonfires in the middle of town streets, filling the chapel with hay, and pilfering fruit from the faculty-only garden (25).

Among that first class of freshmen to graduate from the University of Michigan was one Judson Collins, a young man who, at 14, had joined the Methodist Church during an Ann Arbor revival and who fit in naturally with the religious atmosphere of the early University. In fact, it was a paper assigned to him at school that led him to consider missionary service—in an uncanny coincidence, Collins chose to research Henry Martyn, a man whose missionary work in India and early death would closely prefigure Collins's own life. On graduating from the University in 1845, Collins wrote,

> *Today I took sorrowful leave of many of my old schoolmates, never perhaps to see them again. I never again expect to be circumstanced as I have been here for the last four years. But college days are forever past. The world is before me. I must endeavor by divine will to fulfill well my part in it. (Eva 7)*

Divine will or not, in Collins's first years after graduation, he worked as an instructor at Albion College teaching everything from botany and rhetoric to Greek. Rather than relaxing after the strict schedule imposed by the University of Michigan, he voluntarily increased the rigor of his daily life, waking before dawn at 3:00 or 4:00 AM "to pursue some study and give himself to devotion or preparation for a class or lecture" (Eva 8). He wrote resolutions in his diary to eat less meat and to eat more sparingly at his meals, to devote more time to prayer, and to spend more time in preparation for the next day's work. Given Collins's personality and inclination toward an ascetic life, it's not surprising that even while employed as an instructor, he was working toward a life as a missionary. He submitted an application to the Missionary Board of the Methodist Church and wrote letters to the local bishop requesting an appointment in China, a country that had fascinated Collins during his college years. No one records what sparked this fascination, but one classmate recalled that Collins "searched through every library in the university and the village to find ancient and modern works on China" (Howe). Despite Collins's enthusiasm, the bishop's reply to his inquiry was curt and discouraging: "No mission there—no money to establish one." The Missionary Board's response was not much better: "We have no missions in China. When the Lord wants us to enter China, He will indicate it" (Eva 8).

But Collins was undaunted. In words that were remembered more than a century later by the Methodist Church, Collins replied to the Missionary Board, "Engage me a place before the mast, and my own strong arm will pull me to China and support me while there" (Eva 8). Still, it was some months before he found passage to China, sponsored by a missionary movement at Wesleyan University. A friend recounted the arrival of the commission letter:

Judson Dwight Collins as a young missionary.

I was with him when he heard of the arrival in a distant village. It was dark, and the village was distant. He could hardly stay to "take a piece of bread," and he was on his way for his commission. Before the morning sunlight he had it in his hand. (Hinman 83)

By April 1847, a scant two years after graduating college, Judson Collins set sail for the city of Fuzhou in southeastern China. Boarding a steamer in New York, Collins described in a letter forcing "a passage through a noisy crowd of news boys, peddlers, porters and hack men . . . I found myself safely on board, with time to reflect that I had taken my feet perhaps forever from the soil of my native state." Meeting his two companions, a doctor and his wife, "the three stood at the rail and checked their emotions by singing college songs" (Baker 37).

Four months of travel later, Collins arrived with his companions in southern China's Fujian province. August in the subtropical city of Fuzhou was hot and humid. One million people lived in the city, half of them inside the city walls and half in the suburbs outside. Collins and his companions, the first ever Methodist missionaries in China, were lucky to find housing quickly. An English ship captain offered to rent them his house for $9.00 a month. Situated on an island in the middle of the Min River, the house "looked out on two strong, gracefully-arched bridges sweeping away to . . . the north and south banks of the river" (40). From there, Collins began the first work of his missionary life, handing out religious tracts to throngs of curious city dwellers, many of whom took the tracts in order to write their own notes and receipts in the margins. Less than a year later, Collins and a Chinese teacher had founded a school for children. Eight boys enrolled in classes—half of the day was devoted to Chinese studies and half to the study of Christian writing (51).

Collins's tenure in Fuzhou was not a long one. Amid the rigors of travel, poor sanitation, and the stress of assimilating to a foreign culture, Collins contracted an unnamed illness. Several years after his arrival in China, Collins began the long journey home. At 29 years old, he passed away in his parents' house in Michigan.

A second early graduate of Michigan who made a name for himself by traveling to China was Joseph Beal Steere. He received a BA from the classical school in 1868 and two years later received a degree from the Law School at the University of Michigan. After his graduation in 1870, however, Steere promptly decided to turn his career away from both classics and law. On behalf of the University's burgeoning museum, he agreed to undertake a year-long expedition around the world to gather specimens. Steere, like Judson Collins more than two decades prior, set sail from New York. Unlike Collins, Steere traveled alone—the man who had agreed to be Steere's traveling companion dropped out at the last minute. Seeing the small Gloucester fishing schooner set to carry the two of them to South America, "low in the water, tiny against the pier," Steere's companion reportedly said, "Joe, I'm not good enough for this. I'm going home" ("Joseph Beal Steere" 1).

Battling rough headwinds and choppy seas that "bore them almost as close to the African coast as the South American," the little schooner eventually arrived in Brazil. Steere collected botanical and zoological specimens in Pará and Maranhão, explored the Amazon, and excavated burial mounds on the island of Marajó. During his travels in Brazil, Steere met another young man from the United States, and the two made plans to expedition together. But Steere's misfortune and isolation continued: some weeks later, before they were to rejoin each other's company, Steere received word that his would-be companion had died of yellow fever: "For the rest of the journey, Steere was entirely alone" ("Joseph Beal Steere" 2).

And yet Steere was apparently undaunted by his isolation: from Brazil he traveled to Peru and the Andes and then the Philippines and China. Once in Asia, he spent much of his time in Taiwan, then called Formosa, where he met with indigenous tribes and collected specimens.

Joseph Steere in 1932 on his 90th birthday. Alumni Association Records, Bentley Historical Library, University of Michigan.

All told, Steere's expedition took almost five years. When he returned home in 1875, he was awarded an honorary PhD in zoology and donated some 60,000 botanical, zoological, archaeological, and ethnographic artifacts to the University of Michigan. A collection of this size spurred the University on to invest in its museum, and a short time later, the museum was given its own building to house the newly donated material.

Together, Collins and Steere demonstrate the University of Michigan's early interest in China and are justly remembered as courageous, ambitious students

Joseph Steere (center) with his party of U-M students on an 1887 trip to the Philippines. Joseph Beal Steere Papers, Bentley Historical Library, University of Michigan.

and pioneers in their fields. Yet they also show that the University's early connection to China was that of an institution tentatively reaching across a divide, hoping to learn or convert but not yet embrace. The move toward a more intimate connection between U-M and China began with James B. Angell.

The Tenure and Diplomacy of James Burrill Angell

The University of Michigan that Angell inherited when he took office in 1871 was a far cry from the University that Judson Collins had known just 30 years earlier. The student population had grown from 6 students to more than 1,100; women, at the urging of the Board of Regents, had recently been allowed to enroll; and athletics had become a prominent part of student life, with intramural football and baseball games encouraged by the faculty as a way of venting student energy and curbing vandalism.

Together, Collins and Steere demonstrate the University of Michigan's early interest in China and are justly remembered as courageous, ambitious students and pioneers in their fields.

Angell came to the University as a relatively young man. At 42, he had already served as a professor of modern languages at Brown University, edited the *Providence Gazette*, and served several years as the president of the University of Vermont. It took, apparently, some persuading on the part of the Board of Regents to convince Angell to leave his post at Vermont—in the end, they offered him a salary significantly higher than the previous president of the University and agreed to his stipulation that the President's House be equipped with a bathroom, the first of its kind in Ann Arbor.

When Angell arrived at the University of Michigan, he found that he had landed in no easy position. Troubles with the faculty—low, uncompetitive salaries and overlarge class sizes—were matched by troubles with the students, who had grown unruly and disrespectful during the morning chapel services. The latter issue Angell resolved personally by conducting the chapel service himself and "within the first three days reduced the students to respectful attention." More disruptive to the University's reputation, however, was a controversy that arose just a few years into Angell's tenure. A discrepancy in the funds of a chemistry laboratory was discovered, and the assistant professor, Preston Rose, was accused by his superior of embezzling the money. The controversy became public knowledge, and Rice Beal of the *Ann Arbor Courier* stepped in to defend Rose. Beal, coincidentally, had also helped fund Joseph Steere's expedition around the world, and he "was able to persuade the Regents to buy a half interest in the Beal-Steere collection for the University Museum at the price of their claim against Rose," with the other half of the collection given as a gift (Peckham 75). In the end, Steere's collection of specimens helped resolve a controversy that threw

Steere (right) with L. J. Young. Alumni Association Records, Bentley Historical Library, University of Michigan.

Angell, ca. 1879. James B. Angell Papers, Bentley Historical Library, University of Michigan.

Angell's early years at the University of Michigan into chaos.

With the most difficult years of his tenure behind him, Angell began a new phase of his career that would lead to some of the proudest and happiest times of his life. In February 1880, just as the trouble with the chemistry lab was dying down, Angell received a letter from the US secretary of state, William Evarts. The letter asked for Angell's assistance to help "secure, if possible, a revision of our treaties with that Empire, especially with the purpose of restraining in some degree the emigration which was threatening to flood the Pacific States" (Angell 129).

At the end of the 19th century, as at the start of the 21st, immigration was at the center of a heated debate in the United States. The Burlingame Treaty of 1868 had established China as a "most favored nation," an economic status that guaranteed equal trade advantages between the two countries. But despite this nominal step toward friendly relations, the influx of Chinese immigrants during the Gold Rush and the economic downturn in the United States after the Civil War ignited a conflict that challenged core American values. White supremacy cloaked itself with economic concerns: Chinese immigrants were blamed for low wages and accused of stealing low-paying jobs, and anti-Chinese groups like the Supreme Order of Caucasians formed in California. In 1878, Congress would have passed legislation excluding Chinese if President Hayes had not vetoed the bill.

This was the political atmosphere in which Angell received the letter from Secretary Evarts. Personally, the stakes were also high: the appointment would mean both uprooting his whole family with a move to China and disrupting the University by taking leave from his position as president. When he presented the letter to the Board of Regents, they "were startled, but felt that the University could not afford to miss the honor involved in being second only to Cornell . . . in having its President selected for an important foreign post" (Smith 119). With the regents' blessing, Angell traveled to

Angell working at his desk, 1897. James B. Angell Papers, Bentley Historical Library, University of Michigan.

Washington, DC, to meet with Secretary Evarts and President Hayes. But while Hayes, as Angell wrote in his autobiography, "seemed deeply impressed with the importance of restraining the immigration of Chinese," Angell himself felt some skepticism about the whole project. In a later letter to Evarts, he wrote,

> *The absolute and formal prohibition of the laborers would be diametrically opposed to all our national traditions & would call down the censure of a very large portion, if not a majority, of our most intelligent and high-minded citizens. I must confess that personally I am not ready to favor it, until it is demonstrated much more clearly to me than it now is that the necessity for such a step is overwhelming . . . If the Commission are to be charged with that task, I should prefer that some one else should be appointed in my stead. (Smith 120)*

Angell also expressed skepticism about the economic complaints of the anti-immigrant movement. During a conversation with a labor union representative in California, the representative pushed for Chinese exclusion in order to protect American mechanics. Angell wrote that "I asked him if he could name one mechanic who had been crowded out of employment by the Chinese and he confessed that he could not" (Angell 133).

In the end, Secretary Evarts assured Angell that his misgivings were unnecessary and that the will of the US government was aligned with Angell's position—in other words, Angell was free to work toward a treaty with more nuance than a blanket restriction of Chinese immigration. In short order, Angell was appointed as a minister and a "Chairman of the Commission for revising treaties with China," with John Swift and William Trescot working alongside him as commissioners.

In June 1880, just four months after receiving the letter from Evarts, Angell and his family (he took his wife, daughter, and youngest son) began their travels to China. From

Angell (center) with family outside President's House. James B. Angell Papers, Bentley Historical Library, University of Michigan.

Michigan, they journeyed to San Francisco, sailed to Japan, and finally in late summer arrived in Beijing. All in all, their months of travel by rail and by sea went without mishap, except for a final incident: as the group of travelers sailed up the Pei Ho River from Tianjin to Beijing, both Angell and his daughter, Daisy, reportedly fell overboard. How they fell isn't recorded, and although to a modern reader such a moment sounds comical, falling into a polluted river in the late 19th century could have serious consequences. According to one anecdote, a sea captain who had fallen overboard and swallowed some of the water died of cholera soon after (Smith 130). Angell and his daughter were luckier—they escaped with nothing worse than a humorous story.

Once the party arrived in Beijing, negotiations began in earnest. Prince Gong, uncle to the emperor and head of China's foreign affairs ministry, met with Angell and introduced him to the Chinese commissioners with whom he would be negotiating. Angell, meanwhile, met in private with the other two American commissioners to work out the terms of a newly drafted treaty. Not all went smoothly in their early conversations, however; there was "a sharp difference of opinion" between them. Angell noted that his companion John Swift, a Californian, felt "that we should demand the absolute prohibition of immigration of laborers. Mr. Trescot and I maintained that we should ask merely for a stipulation giving us power to regulate, but not forbid, absolutely, immigration." Swift was outvoted by Trescot and Angell, who, as the chairman of the commission, had the final say. Nevertheless, Swift tried to appeal to a higher power, demanding "that we telephone Mr. Evarts for authority to present his [Swift's] demand. We declined to do so. Mr. Swift, of course, yielded, but not without some feeling" (Angell 142).

Despite the friendly reception the American delegation had received from Prince Gong and the general hospitality they found in Beijing, negotiations between the American and Chinese diplomats got off to a rocky start. As they opened discussion about the first articles in each treaty draft, Angell reports that the American commission "found ourselves so at variance with them, that Mr. Swift declared they did not mean to give us a treaty, and Mr. Trescot, usually so hopeful, thought we had come to the end." Thankfully, Angell "saw the Chinese earnestly discussing and [he] suggested patience" (143). Displaying the same tact and leadership that had charmed both unruly students and the Board of Regents at U-M, Angell suggested working with the last article of the treaty rather than the first and building some common ground. After working through some misunderstandings, everyone "got into the mood of agreeing" and went back to tackle the more difficult material.

On November 17, just 48 days after beginning negotiations, both parties signed the Angell Treaty. "The European ministers were astonished" that the US commission had arrived at a treaty so quickly (Angell 146). It had taken the German minister two years to accomplish something similar, and he had advised Angell that he "must not hope to finish a negotiation under a year" (147). It is difficult to pinpoint the reason for their quick success, whether due to the diplomatic skill of Angell and the Chinese commissioners or some mutual self-interest between the two nations—or, as Angell supposed, the influence on Chinese authorities of his close friend and British diplomat Sir Robert Hart. In any case, with their business concluded, Angell's colleagues Swift and Trescot returned home, leaving Angell to shift positions from chairman of the commission to diplomatic minister.

As minister, Angell's duties were somewhat less charged with tension. He fielded requests from American citizens and missionaries, communicating on their behalf with the Chinese government. But his responsibilities were less difficult than they might have been. In his autobiography, Angell wrote that American missionaries "called on me for help so much more rarely than the British missionaries called on Sir Thomas Wade that he once asked me jocosely if I would not trade missionaries with him" (Angell 163). Angell also kept in close contact with the US government. On one occasion, the secretary of state sent Angell a "very spirited dispatch," writing that a rumor had reached him that the Chinese government planned on seizing the Hawaiian Islands. "It was difficult to make Chinese ministers comprehend the gist of my inquiry," Angell wrote, "but when they did, they burst into a roar of laughter and begged me to inform the Secretary that whenever they formed such a plan they would give the US timely notice" (149).

The end of Angell's period in China left him feeling fond of the friends he had made and proud of the work he had done. With a sentiment surely shared by international students studying at the University of Michigan or American students studying abroad, Angell wrote that "the life at Peking in our time was so remote from the rest of the world that the friendships were very close. It was not without deep emotion that we parted" (Angell 159).

In February 1882, almost exactly two years after receiving the letter from Secretary Evarts, Angell returned home to Ann Arbor and resumed his office as the president of the University. His time in China remained a high point in Angell's life: as his biographer wrote, "there can be little question that [he] always regarded the China episode as the high spot of his career" (Smith 119).

Angell's Legacy

James Angell's reputation as president was impeccable. He shepherded the University through nearly four decades of change, earning a reputation among students for both warmth and toughness. Early in his career, Angell suspended 6 students for hazing. When 81 of their classmates objected, arguing that they were just as guilty as the 6, Angell took them at their word and suspended all 87 of them. He also prided himself on remembering students' names, and every semester, in addition to his administrative duties, Angell insisted on teaching a class on international law. When the head of

Brown University asked Angell for advice on succeeding as a college president, Angell replied, "Grow antennae, not horns" (Smith 356).

Angell's tenure as president at the University of Michigan lasted 38 years, the longest term anyone at U-M has served. He tried to retire twice, but he was so beloved that the Board of Regents refused his first resignation until finally, at age 80, they let him retire. Even though he no longer held office, the board let him live out his days in the President's House on campus.

The consequences of Angell's work as a commissioner and minister to China are more complicated than his legacy at U-M. Just three months after his return to Ann Arbor, and despite Angell's own skepticism on the matter, US president Chester A. Arthur used the Angell Treaty as an opening to sign the Chinese Exclusion Act into law. One of the United States' more shameful pieces of legislation, the Chinese Exclusion Act was the first federal prohibition of an ethnic group. Under the act, Chinese "skilled and unskilled" laborers were prohibited from entering the United States, an intentionally vague category that included most Chinese citizens. "Non-laborers" had to receive documentation from the Chinese government in order to enter, and Chinese already living in the United States were barred from reentry, forcing them to choose between visiting relatives in China and remaining US citizens.

As we'll see in later chapters, the Chinese Exclusion Act caused difficulties for Chinese graduates of the University of Michigan. It wasn't until the alliance between the United States and China during World War II that the act was repealed, which meant that whole generations of prospective students had to deal with the legal challenges of proving that they were not laborers.

Still, Angell's engagement with China opened the door for a relationship between the University and the nation that would flourish in the coming decades. In 1885, for example, "the Chinese

Dr. Angell, 1916. James B. Angell Papers, Bentley Historical Library, University of Michigan.

Angell's funeral, 1916. James B. Angell Papers, Bentley Historical Library, University of Michigan.

government presented to the university its exhibit at the New Orleans Exposition" (Smith 155). The University museum displayed the gifted exhibit for the next 40 years. And after the Boxer Rebellion (1899–1901),

> *the foreign forces consisting of eight countries demanded an indemnity of $333 million from the Chinese government . . . Angell, together with other educators and like-minded people, pushed the US government to return the Boxer Indemnity to China for the establishment of a scholarship program that would allow Chinese students to come to the United States for education. (Bartlet 6)*

Several years later, a Chinese commissioner of education traveling the United States to "determine schools for the indemnity students, placed the University of Michigan among the top five choices" (6).

Since Angell's tenure, the University of Michigan has seen many thousands of Chinese students attend. The following chapters will examine the lives and impact of American students who have followed in Judson Collins's and Joseph Beal's footsteps, those who hope to learn from and to do good in China, as well as Chinese graduates from U-M who walked through doors to international education that James Angell helped open.

Works Cited

Angell, James Burrill. *The Reminiscences of James Burrill Angell*. New York: Longmans, 1912. Print.

Baker, Richard Terrill. *Ten Thousand Years: The Story of Methodism's First Century in China*. New York: Methodist Church Board of Missions and Church Extension, 1947. Print.

Bartlett, Nancy. *The University of Michigan and China: 1845-2008*. Ann Arbor, MI: Bentley Historical Library, 2007. Print.

Eva, Sidney. "Judson Dwight Collins: Missionary from Michigan." Judson Steere Collection, Bentley Historical Library, 1947. Print.

Gaige, Frederick M. "Joseph Beal Steere: Naturalist, Explorer, Educator." Joseph Beal Steere Collection, Bentley Historical Library, 1931. Print.

———. "Michigan Loses Beloved 'Elder Scientist.'" Joseph Beal Steere Collection, Bentley Historical Library, 1941. Print.

Hinman, C. T. *The Model Christian Young Man: An Address on the Life and Character of Rev. Judson Dwight Collins, Late Missionary to China, Delivered before the Union Missionary Society of Inquiry of the University of Michigan, July 14, 1852*. Detroit: Free press book and job office print, 1852. Print.

Howe, E. "The Story of Judson Collins, Missionary." *Detroit Free Press*, 28 July 1901. Print.

Peckham, Howard H. *The Making of the University of Michigan, 1817-1967*. Ann Arbor: U of Michigan P, 1967. Print.

Simpson, Cora. "My Paths Crossed His." *Michigan Christian Advocate*. Judson Steere Collection, Bentley Historical Library, 1947. Print.

Smith, Shirley Wheeler. *James Burrill Angell: An American Influence*. Ann Arbor: U of Michigan P, 1954. Print.

Kang Cheng and Shi Meiyu

The University of Michigan's First Chinese Students

Just 10 years after James Angell returned from his diplomatic work in China, the University of Michigan admitted its first Chinese students. In 1892, Kang Cheng (Ida Kahn) and Shi Meiyu (Mary Stone) traveled from Jiujiang on the southern shores of the Yangtze River to Ann Arbor to take the Medical School's entrance exam. Four years later, they graduated at the top of their class and returned to China, where they opened schools, hospitals, and medical dispensaries. As China entered a period of political uncertainty at the end of the Qing dynasty, Kang Cheng and Shi Meiyu became stabilizing forces in their community. They earned the respect of city elites and the poor alike, embracing a complex identity that was Chinese and Christian and Western all at the same time. They navigated among communities with startlingly different needs and expectations, from fellow missionaries and American congregations to Chinese Nationalist reformers, from government officials and military personnel to the local working poor. Over their lifetimes, Kang and Shi helped create a place of agency and independence for women in New China that emerged at the beginning of the 20th century.

A Michigan Missionary Alone in China

The story of Kang Cheng and Shi Meiyu begins in Ypsilanti, Michigan, with a woman named Gertrude Howe. The daughter of a Quaker family, Howe grew up surrounded by calls to service and social justice. Her father was a staunch abolitionist, and Howe recalled her mother saying to her, "Gertrude, I want you to be something and to do something when you grow up" (Shemo 21). Although Howe enrolled in the Medical School in Ann Arbor, the calling to be a missionary interrupted her education. She joined the Women's Foreign Missionary Society (WFMS) and made plans to travel to India. In the autumn of 1872, Howe made her way to Lansing, Michigan, to receive final instructions. As she gathered together with the other women of the WFMS, however, a telegram came through asking Howe to change her plans and start instead for China the next morning. Howe scrambled to consult with her family—reportedly, her mother was "aghast at this sudden change of plans," but when the morning came, Howe left for China with her father's blessing.

Howe and her traveling companion, Lucy Hoag, found life in Jiujiang, Jiangxi province, to be challenging in their first days. They opened a boarding school for girls, the first of its kind in the Yangtze Valley, but they had difficulty getting anyone to enroll. The city had only become an open-treaty port 10 years prior, and missionaries and foreign teachers were still treated with suspicion. Howe and Hoag "faced rumors that the real reason for their school was to collect the eyes of Chinese children for telescopes and their hearts for medicine," and sometime during their first year in China, locals reportedly attacked and destroyed the school (Shemo 22).

Gertrude Howe as a young missionary. Courtesy of the General Commission on Archives and History, United Methodist Church.

While the school was eventually rebuilt and Howe was unharmed, it's no surprise that she felt lonely and unmoored in Jiujiang. She "jokingly" suggested adopting a daughter to her Chinese language teacher, who took the proposition seriously. Her teacher did, in fact, know of a family with a daughter they couldn't support. Howe stepped in and adopted Kang Aide, to whom she gave the English name Ida Kahn. Over the next decade, Howe would adopt other children, a move that let her create a family even within the strictures of the missionary community and helped her put down roots in China, where she lived until the end of her life.

One of Kang Cheng's constant companions in the WFMS community was Shi Meiyu, the daughter of "impoverished gentry" who became language tutors for the missionaries and themselves eventually converted. Meiyu's father, Shi Ceyu, became the first Chinese Methodist pastor in the Jiangxi province, and it was his idea to begin preparing his daughter for a career as a physician. He proposed to Howe that his daughter receive an education that would prepare her for an American medical school, and although she initially found the idea "startling," Howe soon agreed to arrange English and science classes for Kang and Shi. Shi's reaction to this plan is not recorded, but Kang must have been pleased:

> *When Aide was twelve, [Howe] had found a Chinese man who had traveled overseas and was willing to set up a marriage with his son. According to Howe's later recollection, when she approached Aide about the match Aide "stamped her feet" and refused to marry anyone. She had decided to become a doctor, so she could "help Chinese women like the medical missionaries did." (Shemo 34)*

While contemporary medical programs such as the University of Michigan's integrative medicine initiative find common ground between traditional and scientific medical practices, in the late 1800s, there was a considerable practical and philosophical gulf between traditional Chinese medicine and Western medicine. Even America, at the end of the 19th century, was still slowly adopting Europe's medical advances, such as germ theory. For their whole medical careers, Kang and Shi fought to normalize Western medical practices in China, and they voraciously read recent medical scholarship to keep abreast of new techniques and practices.

Education between Two Cultures: Late 19th Century

Life on the border between American and Chinese traditions made it difficult for Kang and Shi to integrate with other children their age. One issue in particular marked the two girls as different: they didn't bind their feet. While various efforts had been made by the Qing dynasty and others to forbid foot binding, most upper-class and many middle-class girls at the end of the 19th century would still have had bound feet. Kang recalled that at one gathering,

> *the young girls hardly tasted their food, but looked us over from head to foot, especially our feet... Mrs. Stone advised me not to wear spectacles, for I attracted many remarks. I told her I was only too glad to draw attention from our feet. (Shemo 18)*

In another anecdote, Shi was bullied by the other girls in the neighborhood, one of whom "barred her way to school, demanding that Meiyu bow to her own bound feet" (30). In later years, Shi Meiyu's mother even unbound her own feet in support of her daughter, a process just as painful as the initial binding.

For their whole medical careers, Kang and Shi fought to normalize Western medical practices in China.

Howe also made sacrifices for her adopted daughter, living outside the compound that was reserved for foreign missionaries. Shi Meiyu described how, during the sweltering south-central China summers when other missionaries would retreat to foreign-only mountain resorts in Kuling, Howe chose to stay with her adopted children in "a little hut-like home in the hot foothills" (Shemo 27).

In 1892, when Shi was 19 and Kang was 18, they traveled to Ann Arbor to take the University of Michigan's Medical School entrance exam. A Western university would have been, at this time, their only option: while China was beginning to reform its education policies, it would be some time yet before women could receive an equivalent medical degree. Gertrude Howe accompanied the two young women on their journey. The Chinese Exclusion Act (which had replaced the Angell Treaty) was still in effect, and Chinese travelers to the United States were often suspected of being laborers or prostitutes. When immigration officials challenged Kang and Shi, however, the two students had Howe to champion them. Howe drew on influential Methodists in Ann Arbor and contacts at the publication *The Christian Advocate* to help smooth the girls' entry into the United States.

After the rigors of immigration, Kang and Shi had to contend with the entrance exam. In those days, a college education was not a requirement for medical schooling, with the exam serving as proof of a student's eligibility. The entrance exam covered a wide range of subjects, from US history to Latin—it's not hard to imagine the pressure that Kang and Shi must have felt, having traveled around the world for one chance to make their career aspirations a

Shi Meiyu (left) and Kang Cheng as young women. Courtesy of the General Commission on Archives and History, United Methodist Church.

Shi Meiyu (left) and Kang Cheng as students. Courtesy of the General Commission on Archives and History, United Methodist Church.

reality, the two of them among the first Chinese girls to apply to a medical school in the entire United States. In one anecdote,

> Dr. Kahn tells of the difficult entrance examinations and how when she was faced with this question on American history, "Who was the leader of the rebel forces at Gettysburg" that every bit of her cramming for those examinations had left her mind. "But wait!" she said, "Where had I read about the battle until I fairly smelled the smoke on the field and heard the cannons roar? Then everything came back in a vivid flash and I remembered reading Ida Tarbell's 'Life of Abraham Lincoln' and I quickly jotted down 'General Lee.'" (Shemo 45)

Both Kang and Shi passed their exams with high marks and began their lives at the University of Michigan.

For the first two years of school, Howe stayed in the United States, living with Kang and Shi to help ease their transition. While both women continued to excel in school, in an interview many years later, Howe recalled that "the terrible terrors of the laboratory" gave the two students sleepless nights. Shi herself said that "life in America was a different world to us and the Medical Language was a different language" (Shemo 46). In the face of such academic rigor and cultural transition, another pair of students might have clung together for support and, understandably, had difficulty engaging with the other students. Not Kang and Shi. After the first two years, Howe left them on their own to board with a woman named Mrs. Frost, who recalled them having many friends whom they would sometimes invite over for "a little Chinese feast." The two wore American-style clothes, and in her junior year, Kang was elected as the secretary for her class (46).

Four years after being shepherded to the United States by Gertrude Howe, Kang Cheng and Shi Meiyu graduated with distinction. Many accounts, in fact, place them as the top second and third students of their class (though none of the sources indicate who was second and who was third). On the day of their graduation ceremony, rather than wear a cap and gown, Kang and Shi wore traditional Chinese garments, Kang in a blue silk robe, Shi in pink. They were the first Chinese women to attend the University of Michigan, and there they were, receiving a diploma from James Angell while wearing symbols of their homeland.

Putting Down Roots at the End of the Qing Dynasty

Kang and Shi returned to Jiujiang in 1896, serving, as Howe did, with the WFMS. Howe and others suggested that the two graduates spend a few years training with established hospitals in Shanghai, but Kang and Shi rejected this plan, perhaps wanting to prove that their education had been preparation enough for the work of providing medical care. In any case, they didn't waste much time—shortly after arriving, they opened a small medical dispensary for women. And despite concerns from the WFMS that the dispensary would have difficulty getting off the ground, three days after opening, four patients presented themselves for treatment. Soon Kang and Shi were running a thriving operation. They described one particularly difficult case in which a mother giving birth to twins had ceased labor after the delivery of the first child. The family sent for Kang and Shi, who were able to save the lives of both the mother and the second child, although the first child died. Once the mother had recovered, the family threw a feast for the two physicians and, in the evening, "[followed] them home with fireworks" (Shemo 50).

Shi Meiyu the year of her graduation, 1896. BMC Media Services records, Bentley Historical Library, University of Michigan.

Some of the challenges of opening a practice in Jiujiang came, in fact, not from the Chinese locals but from the missionary society. While neither Kang nor Shi took a salary for the first few years in order to repay school funding provided by the WFMS, when they did start receiving a salary, it was substantially lower than what their non-Chinese counterparts were making. But there was an even more visible inequality: they weren't allowed to live in the nicely appointed missionary compound. The strict Chinese-foreign segregation was enforced even for Kang and Shi. In the coming years, this hypocrisy would become increasingly embarrassing for the WFMS as Kang and Shi's prestige grew. Their very presence encouraged the missionary institution to reexamine its values and policies.

By 1898, Kang and Shi were already lobbying to expand their practice into a full-size hospital. Fundraising letters sent by Shi Meiyu described their current working conditions as "crammed full . . . fairly an oven," and she was hoping "for signs or signals from the women of America to build our new hospital" (Shemo 61). With financial support from Dr. I. N. Danforth, a physician mentor Shi had met in Chicago, by 1900, the new building was complete, described as "airy[,] . . . plentifully supplied with comfortable verandahs" and full of modern appliances (62).

"Entrance to Danforth Memorial Hospital. Kiukiang, China." Courtesy of the General Commission on Archives and History, United Methodist Church.

The satisfaction of opening the new hospital was short lived. When Kang and Shi returned to China in 1896, the political climate, though turbulent, welcomed them as ambitious women who might help revitalize what many saw, after the disastrous Sino-Japanese War, as a Chinese population sapped of strength. One famous scholar and reformist, Liang Qichao, even wrote an essay on Kang Cheng in which he praised her as a model of the "New Woman" of China. Just four years later, however, the Boxer Rebellion had gained enough momentum that Kang and Shi's lives as missionaries in Jiujiang were threatened. With the slogan "Support the Qing, Destroy the Foreign," by early 1900, Boxers began attacking and killing missionaries in northern China. The Qing government, caught between a shared antiforeign resentment with the Boxers and binding treaty agreements with those same foreign powers, was slow to condemn the attacks.

While the most violent expressions of the Boxer Rebellion remained in northern China, the movement continued to grow in central and southern China. By the summer of 1900, the threat had spread, and while the Qing governors-general remained in control of the cities, it was unclear how many officials sympathized with the Boxers. Kang and Shi's practice, meanwhile, suffered: "Through fear our patients had dwindled away until we only had a few every day," Shi wrote. Shortly thereafter, they were forced to abandon their new hospital entirely when the American consul ordered all women and children to leave Jiujiang. Howe, Kang, Shi, and many others boarded ships for Japan, where they would take refuge until the end of the year. Although the hospital itself remained unscathed during the uprising, Shi's father died from wounds he sustained during an attack (Shemo 63). A letter from Kang written during this period shows her love and concern for her country:

> *Sometimes my heart aches so much for my people, and crying does not even relieve me, until I throw myself completely at my Savior's feet, realizing that He also cares and will comfort His poor afflicted children everywhere. I suppose this had to come before a new China could be brought forth, but oh, at what a cost.* (64)

Neither Kang nor Shi saw any conflict between their Christianity and their nationalism. And while this put them in the company of leaders such as Sun Yat-sen and Chiang Kai-shek, for whom Christianity was an avenue of reform and political advancement, Kang and Shi melded the two with no indication that one might diminish the other.

Diverging Paths: Shi Meiyu and Conflict with the Missionary Society

After nearly a decade of working as partners in Jiujiang, Kang and Shi's paths diverged. A group of gentry in the province's capital, Nanchang, invited Kang to establish a medical practice in their city. In 1903, Kang accepted their invitation, and although the two women parted on good terms, they would never again work side by side at a hospital.

Shi Meiyu remained in Jiujiang, now shouldering twice the workload. Her old mentor, Dr. Danforth, worried that the task would be too difficult alone and offered to find an American nurse who might be willing to help out. Shi refused. More important than her own health was her hospital's autonomy as a Chinese-run institution. She felt "determined to present her hospital as a model of Chinese women developing a medical ministry without Western supervision" (Shemo 72).

The next several years would bring some significant life changes for Shi. Her sister, Anna, returned from studies in the United States to help Shi with the management of the missionary aspects of the hospital, despite having been diagnosed with tuberculosis. And the hospital continued to grow in fame, with Shi herself a draw for guests. One report mentions "one progressive official" who "wished his daughter to take a journey of 450 miles to see Dr. Stone for the inspiration she would receive." Despite this reputation, Shi and her sister still lived outside the WFMS missionary compound in "a tiny rented native hut" (Shemo 74). In 1906, Anna succumbed to her illness. In less than a decade, Shi had lost both her father and her sister.

In the midst of this turmoil, Shi Meiyu received a blessing. Jennie Hughes, an American missionary who had fled to Jiujiang from the capital during the Boxer Rebellion, arrived to take over some of Anna's duties, teaching classes and organizing the evangelistic outreach.

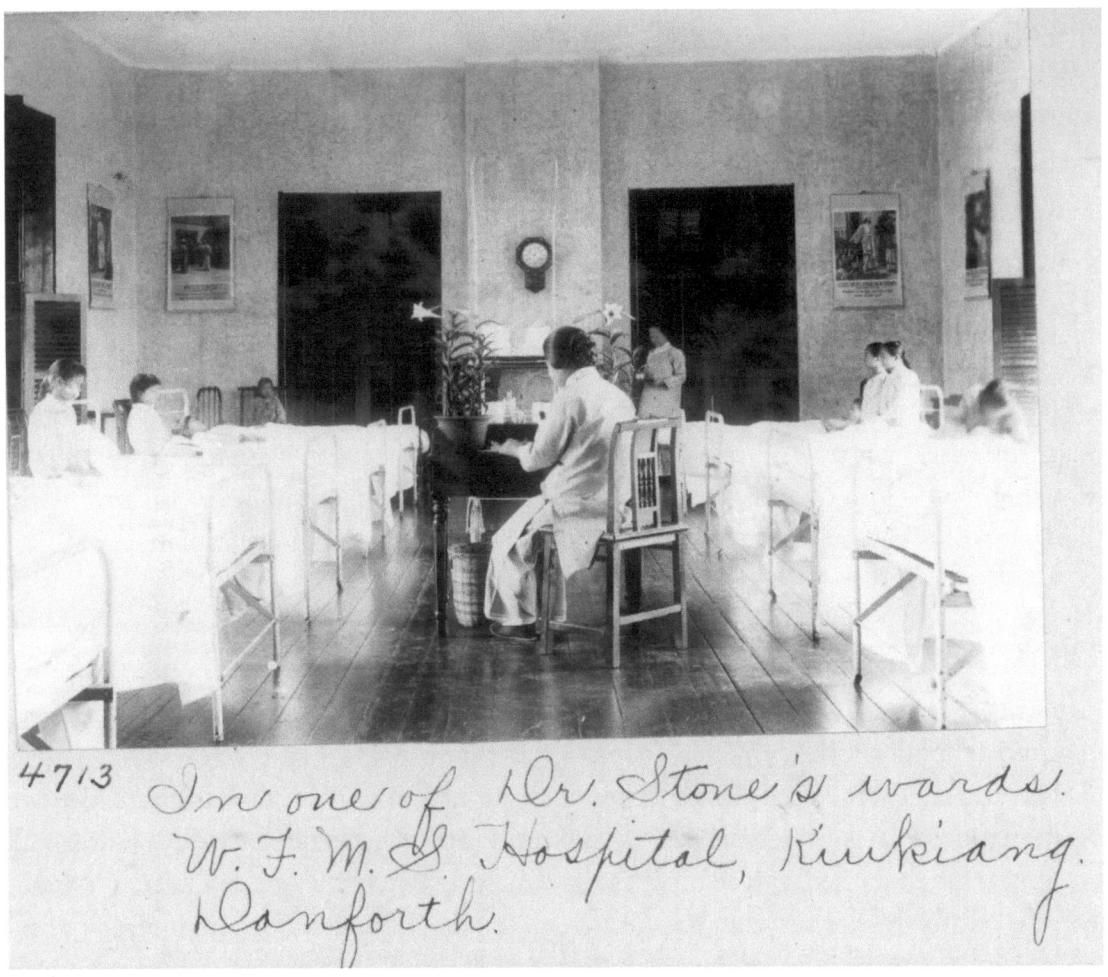

"In one of Dr. Stone's wards. WFMS Hospital, Kiukiang. Danforth." Courtesy of the General Commission on Archives and History, United Methodist Church.

Soon Jennie had moved into Shi's house in Anna's place, and there she would remain for the rest of her life as Shi's companion and life partner. Dr. Danforth, meeting the couple years later in Chicago, said "the harmony—may I not say Christian love—existing between Miss Hughes and Dr. Stone is something worth going a long way to see" (75).

Shi's vision for Jiujiang and China wasn't limited to the creation of a functioning hospital. While most missions taught English and religion classes, Shi started a nursing school too. At a time when infant mortality was high, Shi hoped that Western obstetrics could supplement traditional midwifery. She also trained her nurses in basic surgical skills. In the rare weeks that Shi and Jennie were away from the hospital, she had such faith in her nurses' abilities that Shi trusted them to cover all of her ordinary duties.

The nursing program gave the women who joined agency and options. One anecdote describes a nurse, Ho Yin, who reversed traditional gender roles and supported both her fiancé and her brothers after their father passed away. Another anecdote recounts a man bringing his wife to the hospital hoping that Shi would certify the woman as mentally unstable in order to facilitate a divorce. Shi refused, and when the man abandoned his wife at the hospital, Shi offered the woman a position in the nursing school. The school and hospital became a "haven for women who needed an independent means of support," providing an alternative to marriage and a safety net for those who needed it.

In 1906, Jennie and Shi traveled to the United States. Shi needed to have her appendix removed, but maybe even more urgently, she needed rest. She had been working at a feverish pace for more than a decade and was still reeling from the deaths of her sister and father. At the time, the Chinese Exclusion Act restricted the immigration of Chinese laborers. Entering the United States had become a nightmare for Chinese citizens;

"Patients waiting to enter clinic at Danforth Memorial Hospital. Kiukiang." Courtesy of the General Commission on Archives and History, United Methodist Church.

even those travelers exempted from the act often had to undergo "Kafkaesque drama" at Angel Island, where they might be interrogated by immigration officers intending to trick them into admitting that they were laborers. So when, as they landed in San Francisco, a tugboat approached their ship and the officer aboard asked for a Chinese woman named Stone, it is no surprise that Shi's "heart was like lead" (Shemo 89). But instead of interrogating and deporting her, the officer told them that President Teddy Roosevelt himself, informed of Shi's travel plans by the WFMS, had sent the ship for them directly.

What began as a furlough for rest and recovery from appendicitis soon became a speaking tour of the United States. Shi and Jennie traveled across the country, speaking at colleges, churches, women's groups, and social clubs in the hope of raising funds for their medical work. Soon Shi garnered a reputation as a charismatic, persuasive speaker. She adopted American slang, wore "a Chinese silk jacket and an American style skirt," and spoke so passionately that "no one could resist [her] persuasive tones," and "not once did she fail to get what she asked for" (Shemo 91–92). By the time her tour of the United States was over, Shi had raised enough money to expand the medical practice considerably and build herself and Jennie a proper house.

Their practice continued to expand in the following decade: the hospital developed its nursing program, and the mission's Bible school for girls grew, under Jennie Hughes's direction, to include what was essentially a full high school curriculum, one that was capable of training young women to the point of eligibility for higher education. But their practice expanded too much for the comfort of the WFMS, and by 1920, some friction developed between the group and Jennie Hughes over the kind of education students at the Bible school should receive.

This tension, combined with continued income inequality between foreign and Chinese workers, proved too much, and in the early 1920s, both Shi and Jennie resigned from the WFMS, resolving instead to create an independent mission that could live up to their ideals. After several years of fundraising, they founded the Bethel mission, a compound in Shanghai that included a hospital, a nursing school (which attracted as many as 200 students a year), a high school, and a chapel.

Here they worked until World War II. When the Japanese began bombing Shanghai in 1937, Shi Meiyu and Jennie Hughes happened to be traveling in northern China. There they received telegrams urging them to not return to Bethel but to flee instead to Hong Kong. They followed this advice and, in the end, sailed all the way from Hong Kong to Pasadena, California. Shi and Hughes would live together in the United States through the end of the war and for the rest of their lives, overseeing the reconstruction of the Bethel mission from afar. Jennie Hughes died in 1951, and Shi Meiyu followed three years later, passing away in 1954.

Shi Meiyu in her years as a physician. Bentley Historical Library, University of Michigan.

Kang Cheng: An Accidental Diplomat at the Birth of a New China

Kang Cheng and Shi Meiyu parted ways in 1903, when Kang, on the invitation of the city elite, moved to Nanchang with Gertrude Howe in order to start a new medical practice. There Kang found a much different culture than the one she'd left behind in Jiujiang. While Nanchang was the capital of the province, it was also far less exposed to Western influence than Jiujiang, which had been a treaty port city since the middle of the 19th century. She recalled a visit to the city back in 1898 during the swelling antiforeign sentiment before the Boxer Rebellion. A crowd had surrounded her and her traveling companion, an American WFMS missionary, and while her American friend was allowed through, the crowd threw stones at Kang and taunted her with jeers of

"A foreigner! A foreigner!" When she tried to enter a house to escape the barrage, she found the gate barred against her. Luckily, more sympathetic members of the crowd helped her escape (Shemo 103).

Things weren't quite so bad when Kang returned to Nanchang in 1903. She established a small medical dispensary with funds from the local elite, and yet, for all the interest the gentry and reformists showed in Kang, there was an equal disinterest from the city's ordinary citizens. This disparity is visible in the numbers: "In her first year, Kang saw just over 2000 patients, as opposed to the more than 12000 that Shi and her nurses treated in Jiujiang" (Shemo 109). And Kang herself gave voice to the frustration of dealing with a skeptical population:

> *Can you imagine your sensations if patient after patient to whom you were called were clothed in their best official garments and were then laid out... ready to breathe their last? That was the situation I faced in this huge old town of Nanchang simply because it had no people who believed in Western medicine. No wonder my servant said I had no talent, and I was ready to believe it too, for how could I revive these dying women? (109)*

Even when the number of patients increased, Kang's first years in Nanchang were marked with anxiety and financial troubles. Gertrude Howe and her sister gave Kang what money they could, and Kang even sold "her little stock of jewelry" to help pay for the expensive rent and the medicines she distributed daily. In a later written work, she described those years, saying, "The anxiety as well as the financial hardship was almost too much to be borne" (Shemo 110).

Gradually, however, support for Kang's work grew among the gentry and the Methodist missionary community. Some members of the gentry purchased the land to build a hospital in addition to the dispensary—a property within the walls of Nanchang itself and the only missionary community with that distinction. And a short time later, a visiting Methodist bishop was reportedly dismayed to find a physician of such renown living inside the crowded dispensary. Returning home, the bishop diverted $5,000 to build a home nearby for Kang and Howe.

Growth came more rapidly in the 1910s. Kang and Howe, like Shi several years before, conducted a fundraising tour of the United States, and they returned to Nanchang to find their hospital completed. The revolution of 1911 and the overthrow of the Qing dynasty inspired in many citizens the hope of reform and the prospect of building a new Chinese Republic. Western ideals became in Nanchang both more familiar and more favorable. When the political philosopher, activist, and architect of the revolution Sun Yat-sen came through Nanchang in 1912, Kang had enough prestige among the elite to throw a banquet in his honor. Sun Yat-sen himself observed Kang's work and donated some money toward the running of the hospital. In the months after receiving such a resounding seal of approval, Kang experienced a sharp upswing in the number of patients interested in her hospital.

The idealism of the 1911 revolution gave way to a period of uncertainty at the end of the decade and into the 1920s. The dream of a unified republic failed to materialize, and in its place came a long period of warlordism, during which the country fractured into provinces and cities under the control of independent leaders. Luckily for Kang, the governor of Nanchang was sympathetic to her work. Elsewhere, Nationalist sentiment continued to grow as the Guomindang (GMD; Kuomintang) Party, founded by Sun Yat-sen, sought to unify a splintered China. Foreign elements, including missionaries and Chinese Christians, were branded as imperialists. Kang found herself having to balance a series of complicated loyalties to her faith and church, to the local government and the soldiers who needed medical care, and to the GMD troops looking to end the era of warlordism.

Because of these complexities, Kang was forced to compromise, letting soldiers rest in her compounds and allowing her female nurses to treat male patients, an issue that in the past had caused friction between her and the WFMS. The pressure on her to perform under politically fraught circumstances also increased. One anecdote describes one of the highest-ranking officials in Nanchang summoning Kang to treat a member of his family. The ailing woman had already been seen by practitioners of traditional medicine, who had refused to treat her due to the severity of her illness. "The least mistake in diagnosis, and she would be dead," wrote Kang. "Fear filled my heart." She too was unable to make a clear diagnosis, but under pressure from the official and his family, she prescribed some medicines anyway: "I thought how incapable I was, and how little I knew! I wished I had never tried to be a doctor" (Shemo 237). Despite Kang's reservations, the woman made a startling and rapid recovery, and thereafter Kang was trusted to treat other members of the family.

When she wasn't directly helping the wounded, Kang offered her hospital compound as a sanctuary. Two stories high with a central courtyard, a green lawn, and a garden of fruit trees and flowers cultivated by Kang herself, the compound served as a shelter for "terror stricken women, men, and children" fleeing from the combat between warlords and the Guomindang. While soldiers looted many other homes, they left Kang's untouched, perhaps due to her connections with the elite of Nanchang or because of her connection to a foreign mission. Despite anti-imperialist sentiments, combatants were reluctant to provoke armed responses from foreign powers. Kang flew the American flag above her hospital, saying, "You may speak all you wish of extraterritoriality, but if the 'Stars and Stripes' could save these poor women and children from being terror stricken, then I am glad we could borrow this protection" (Shemo 241).

Kang took extra steps toward diplomacy by inviting high-ranking officers and generals from both sides to banquets at her house so that they might have "a more favorable (or less unfavorable) view of Christianity" and "leave us alone." Kang's house and name became "a talisman throughout the city," a byword for safety. When, in the autumn of 1926, the Guomindang finally took control of Nanchang, Kang retained her connections with the party. Officers still came to dinner at her house and, she hoped, "would go away feeling decidedly more friendly, and not so cocksure about the evils of Christianity" (242).

The peace didn't last. In the spring of the following year, GMD troops attacked American, British, and Japanese embassies in Nanjing. In retaliation and to provide cover for fleeing civilians, American and British destroyers fired on the city. The resentment of foreigners among Chinese soared. A month passed until Kang and Gertrude Howe (by now suffering from Alzheimer's) woke up one morning to find their mission compound deserted. All foreign missionaries, with the exception of Howe, had arranged to leave Nanchang in secret. No one had told Kang. A servant came with a note explaining what had happened and that the plan was to have been "strictly confidential among the foreigners" (Shemo 244).

Kang Cheng, or Ida Kahn as she was known in America, during her years as a physician. Barbour Scholarship for Oriental Women Committee Records, Bentley Historical Library, University of Michigan.

To the missionary community, Kang must not have been "American enough" to take into confidence, and the lack of trust must have felt like betrayal. Even more difficult to forgive would have been the abandonment of Howe. Knowing that Kang would never leave her adoptive mother, the American consul and other missionaries chose to leave Howe behind rather than invite Kang. Kang herself described the experience: "We woke up one morning to find that all our missionaries had left, apparently without sending one word to us. I can never describe the pain of that moment."

Being left alone, without the protection of the foreign community, put Kang and Howe in considerable danger. Other missionary hospitals were burned and looted; "Chinese pastors suffered beatings and kidnappings" (Shemo 245). Nonetheless, Kang remained in Nanchang, and while her home was never destroyed, soldiers invaded the compound, using her lawn as a drilling yard and stripping her carefully planted garden of fruit. She was, in other words, harassed by the same Nationalist army that had once dined at her home and been treated at her hospital. Officers lectured her and her nurses, calling them "the running dogs of foreigners." Kang's nurses, however, refused to applaud, and Kang herself stood up to defend herself, applying Sun Yat-sen's "Three Principles" to their medical work, arguing that "we are true Nationalists" (245).

For the next several years, even after Howe's death in 1928, Kang protested vocally against the threat of the Chinese Communist Party, which was now taking refuge in her province, and later against the Japanese invasion of Manchuria. She wrote essays calling for aid from the international community even as she struggled to maintain funding for her hospital in the embattled Jiangxi province.

By the end of 1931, Kang herself had fallen gravely ill. One missionary described cancer in the abdomen, "which had spread down into her legs until one of her thigh bones broke." Others described liver disease and kidney failure: "It is clear that Kang was in a great deal of pain before her death" (Shemo 253). Still she managed to treat others up until the end, even being carried up and down stairs to visit patients. When Kang realized that she was dying, she called for Shi Meiyu, who came to visit one final time. The two "sang hymns and other songs they had learned as children" (254).

A Legacy of Selflessness

Their names are no longer widely known, and their stories are not widely taught. And yet Kang Cheng and Shi Meiyu have left a clear legacy: in China, they introduced a whole province to Western medical practices, began a modern nursing education system that continues today, inspired reformists to imagine new roles for women as China shed its dynastic traditions, and personally tended to many thousands of the sick and injured in Jiujiang and Nanchang.

At the University of Michigan, Kang and Shi have left a lasting, if indirect, mark—they met Levi Barbour, a regent for the University, and their example inspired him to create the Barbour Scholarship for Oriental Women, which will be the focus of the next chapter.

Works Cited

Burton, Margaret E. *Notable Women of Modern China*. New York: Fleming H. Revell, 1912. Print.

Izant, Edwin. "Excerpts from a Talk Honoring Gertrude Howe." Lansing, MI: Central Methodist Church, 1947. Print.

Shemo, Connie Anne. *The Chinese Medical Ministries of Kang Cheng and Shi Meiyu, 1872–1937: On a Cross-Cultural Frontier of Gender, Race, and Nation*. Bethlehem: Lehigh UP, 2011. Print.

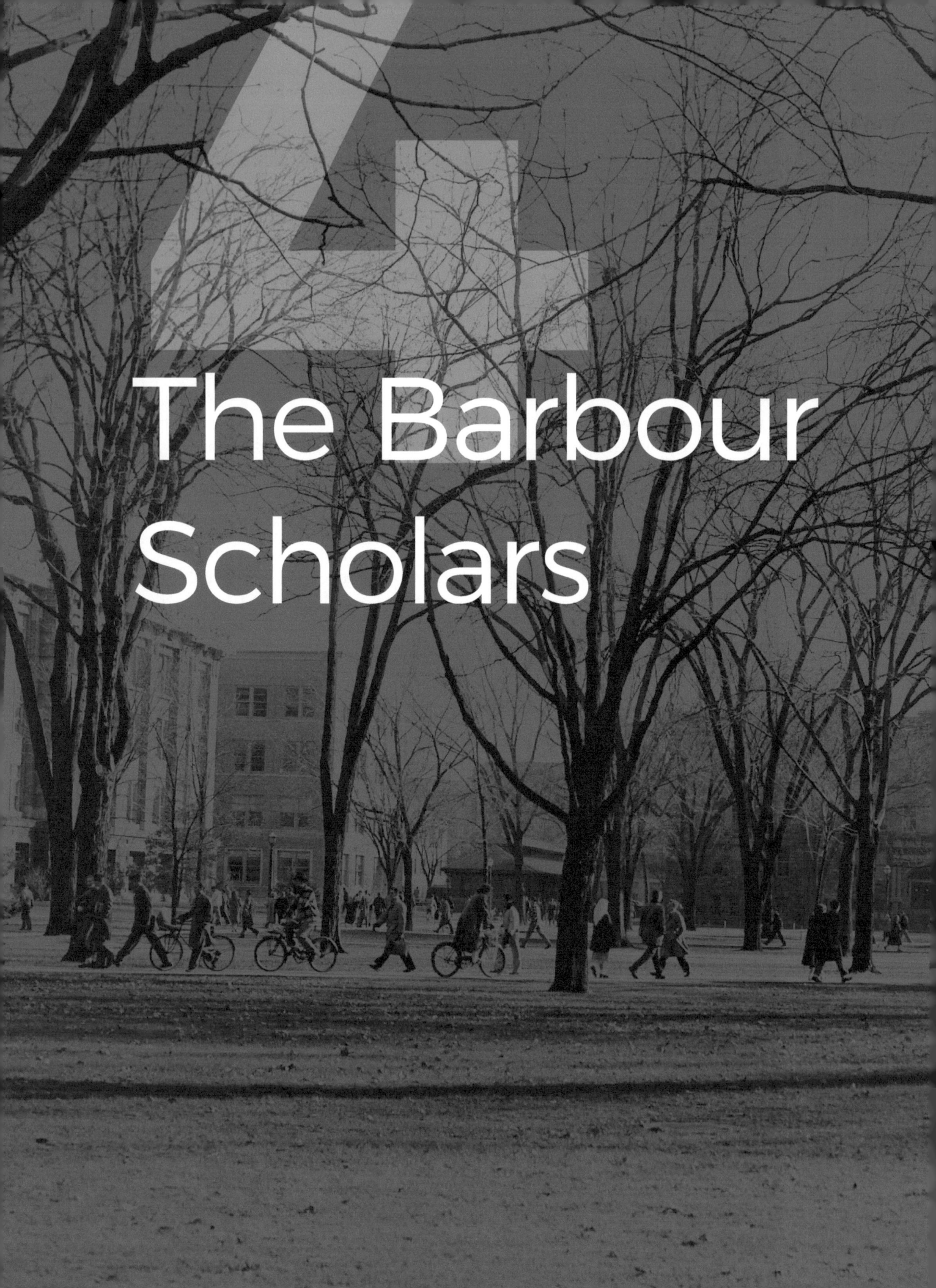

4. The Barbour Scholars

In 1917, some 20 years after the graduation of Kang Cheng and Shi Meiyu, the University of Michigan (U-M) made its first formal overtures of welcome to women from Asian countries with the Barbour Scholarship. Founded and funded by Levi Lewis Barbour, a graduate of U-M and a regent for the University, the scholarship invited qualified women to study at Michigan and then return to their home countries enriched with their newly acquired knowledge. As Barbour himself put it in a letter to U-M President Harry Burns Hutchins in 1919, the idea of the scholarship "was to bring girls from the Orient, giving them an Occidental education, and let them take back whatever they found good, and assimilate the blessings among the people from which they might come."

To date, more than 700 women from India to Turkey to China have come to the University of Michigan supported by either the Barbour Scholarship or (for advanced degrees) the Barbour Fellowship. In the early years of the program, women from China made up the majority of the scholarship recipients. For many of these women, the Barbour Scholarship proved to be a springboard into positions of power and authority at home in China, making space for women in traditionally male-dominated institutions. While there are too many such examples to cover in a single chapter or book, this chapter will tell the story of Levi Barbour and two of the most impressive leaders—Ding Maoying (Ting Me-Iung) and Wu Yifang—who owed their success in medical and educational institutions in part to Barbour's philanthropy.

Levi Barbour attended the University of Michigan during its fledgling years. Born in 1840 in Monroe, Michigan, Barbour received a BA in 1863 and a law degree two years later. From the earliest years of his career, Barbour seems to have been oriented toward charity and social justice. After passing the bar exam and marrying Ann Arbor local Harriet Hooper, Barbour settled in Detroit as a junior partner at a law firm in 1866.

Barbour worked hard to develop the city, playing "a leading role in the purchase of Belle Isle for the park system." He also "organized a secular agency, the Association of Charities, a forerunner of the United Way, and served as its first president" (Faerber 20).

But of all the social issues that concerned Barbour, the accessibility of college education was perhaps the most important to him. In 1897, a decade after Angell returned from China and the year after Kang Cheng and Shi Meiyu's graduation from the University of Michigan, Barbour published an essay called "College Training for Professional Men." Tellingly, the essay opens with this line: "I can fancy but one broader or more important topic of discussion before an audience of college men than this, and that would be 'College Training for Everybody'" (Barbour 1). Later, Barbour wrote that he hoped college education would someday be as universal and accessible as primary school—a core value that inspired much of his philanthropic work.

The struggle to allow women to attend the University of Michigan must have been fresh in Barbour's mind. As a student himself in the mid-1860s, female students would have been allowed to receive a co-ed high school education but not participate in university classes.

In 1858, a committee of regents produced a divided report on the appropriateness of higher education for women, and while then president Henry Philip Tappan "strongly approved of higher education for young women . . . he advocated for separate facilities and curricula," believing that "women were physically and intellectually incapable of competing with men in the college environment" (Faerber 5). It wasn't until 1870 that, prodded by the state legislature, U-M changed its policies and admitted its first female student.

When Barbour began his first term as regent at the end of the

Portrait of Levi L. Barbour. Barbour Scholarship for Oriental Women Committee Records, Bentley Historical Library, University of Michigan.

19th century, it's no surprise that he and President Angell became close friends as well as colleagues. Both men shared a belief in women's suffrage and in the importance of making a university education accessible to women. Barbour "worked closely with President Angell in enthusiastically implementing the Board's policy admitting women to the University with equal privileges," and together they established the University's first dean of women position, filled by Dr. Eliza Mosher. During these years, Barbour made a gift of land in Detroit to the University, the sale of which was used to build the Barbour Gymnasium, a center for women's activities on campus.

Although it took several years after his 1913 tour of Asia to get the scholarship officially off the ground, Barbour wasted no time in implementing the principles of the fund. In 1914, he invited two Japanese women to study in the United States. Barbour paid their expenses, hired tutors, and even housed them in his own home for their first few months. By 1917, after several years' worth of preparation with President Hutchins, a formal proposal to the board of regents, and a donation of some $55,000, the Barbour Scholarship was officially implemented. That year, one Gladys Ding Chen from China became the first official Barbour Scholar.

From 1917 until his death eight years later, Barbour shepherded the program. He doubled the endowment, helped manage and revise the program's policies, and gifted several rental properties to the University so that the program might be self-sustaining (Faerber 23). When he learned that one student had contracted tuberculosis due to inadequate living conditions, Barbour built a new residence hall for women on campus. Named after his mother, a lifelong role model for Levi, the Betsy Barbour House still stands on Ann Arbor's central campus today. When Barbour passed away in 1925, he left the furniture from his own household to the Betsy Barbour Residence Hall and the entirety of his homestead to the scholarship program.

Levi Barbour devoted himself to the cause of making education accessible to everyone, particularly women. As I'll explore in the rest of the chapter, Barbour's investment in the ability and promise of Chinese women has paid immense dividends.

Ding Maoying: Hospital Director, Aid Worker, and National Representative

One such Michigan graduate was Ding Maoying. Ding attended the University of Michigan twice, receiving a medical degree in 1920 and returning eight years later for a Barbour Fellowship. Over the course of her career, Ding became a director of the Tianjin Women's Hospital, the head of the Chinese delegation to the Pan-Pacific Women's Conference in Honolulu, and the author of one of the earliest books on prenatal care for mothers in China.

Gathering of Chinese students at a Barbour program ball. Bentley Historical Library, University of Michigan.

Professor Frank L. Huntley (left), secretary of the Barbour program beginning in 1946, with his wife (center) and Chiang Kai-shek, generalissimo of the Nationalist forces in China. Bentley Historical Library, University of Michigan.

The story of Ding's extraordinary career begins at the McTyeire Missionary School in Shanghai. There she met Tsao Li Tsuin, a student several years older, who became a mentor and friend and encouraged Ding's interest in medicine. Soon this friendship—and Ding's future—was tested. Rather than allow his daughter to complete her education, Ding's father had betrothed her to "a sickly, older friend of his" (Ting). Sources differ on how she escaped. Some say she ran to the missionaries for help, while her great-niece Evelyn Kay Ting thinks it more likely that her friend Tsao Li Tsuin helped her escape. Either way, Ding fled marriage and made her way to America.

In the United States, Ding finished her undergraduate degree at Mount Holyoke College before enrolling in the University of Michigan Medical School. During her time in Ann Arbor, Ding began to exchange letters with Dr. Abby Turner, an instructor from Mount Holyoke who would go on to become a lifelong correspondent and confidant. These letters survive today, and they provide windows into Ding's experiences as a student in America and as a doctor in China. Ding described, for example, taking a summer course in experimental physiology with one Dr. Cope, who devoted "his whole time to students." Ding wrote that she thought that it was "just as good a course as you can get in this country." She also enjoyed Ann Arbor in the summertime: "There are many beautiful shady trees. There are good many places for long walks and recreation. Barbour gymnasium is opened to all summer school students. There is a small swim pool and many showers" (letter ca. 1919–1920).

Portrait of Ding Maoying. Alumni Association Records, Bentley Historical Library, University of Michigan.

But as much as Ding immersed herself in her studies at Michigan, her home country was never far from her mind. As she wrote in 1919, a year before her graduation,

> *I will do what is the best for my people in China. There are few who are fortunate as I to be able to study abroad. There are many physicians in China who have no*

Envelope of a letter Ding sent to Dr. Abby Turner. Courtesy of Donna Albino, http://www.mtholyoke.edu/~dalbino.

business to be. After my years training I ought be able to do some thing for my people. Dr. Tsao wants me to help her. After all the only thing I want to do is to give my whole self to my country. (Letter 1919)

Dr. Tsao, Ding's old friend from the McTyeire Missionary School, was now herself a practicing physician. When Ding graduated with an MD in 1920, she spent two years interning in hospitals and gaining practical experience; in 1922, after nearly a decade abroad, Ding returned home to China. The poverty and war of the early 1920s, a result of the period of warlordism that followed the fall of the Qing dynasty, must have been a surprise. "There is fighting in [the] northern part of Chi-li," Ding wrote. "We people have nothing to do with it. These war-lords will eventually kill themselves. That will be the salvation of China. I am happy that I took a training home to help my people" (June 1922). And Ding was able to reunite with her father, despite her disruption of the betrothal that he had arranged. "My father was so proud of me," she wrote in the same letter. "It certainly was a happy homecoming."

Unfortunately, this happiness was not to last even as long as the summer. On August 11, 1922, Ding prepared to take her friend Dr. Tsao out for dinner. But as Li Tsuin Tsao started to dress, she complained of a headache. "She suffered only five

Ding Maoying in Ann Arbor, ready to graduate in 1920. Courtesy of Donna Albino, http://www.mtholyoke.edu/~dalbino.

Ding at the YWCA in Shanghai, ca. 1918. Archives and Special Collections, Mount Holyoke College.

minutes and went sound asleep until her last breath," Ding wrote. Dr. Tsao died of a cerebral hemorrhage just three days later. With Dr. Tsao's sister having also passed away just weeks before, Ding was left alone in Tianjin: "Within three weeks, two of my best friends left me . . . Everything is like a dream to me now" (September 1922).

The heavy workload at the Peiyang Women's Hospital in Tianjin, however, gave Ding no time to grieve. With Dr. Tsao gone, much of the workload and authority fell on Ding. "Work is too heavy for a young doctor," Ding wrote. "I would like to have ~~enough~~ more time to read up my cases. I did my own laboratory work also. Since the death of Dr. Tsao I had to have charge of hospital account" (September 1922). The crossed-out *enough* is particularly poignant—Ding, so overwhelmed by work, wished only for more time, not enough time. In the same letter, she gives some sense of the particulars of her burden: "Within three months I have seen three thousand patients at clinic, delivered forty five babies, operated ten times, made sixty calls outside." No wonder that Ding longed for the comparatively easygoing life at Michigan just two years before: "I miss my college life. I would give anything if I could just get away for a good walk in the woods" (September 1922).

THE BARBOUR SCHOLARS   45

Ding in her back yard in Tianjin, 1922. Courtesy of Donna Albino, http://www.mtholyoke.edu/~dalbino.

Nonetheless, Ding felt it was her duty to carry on Dr. Tsao's "unfinished task," as she called it. Ding was forced to deal with the challenges of being in a position of authority while still so young: "It is the hospital management that tries my temper. Being young in experience I often would not know how to deal with people" (December 1922). For the next eight years, Ding persevered and built up the hospital, hiring additional doctors and nurses, sending others to America for training, and expanding the hospital's technical capacities. Armed conflict among Nationalists, Communists, and local warlords was a perpetual concern. In the winter of 1924, Ding wrote that civilians "would not dare to be on [the] streets at night in October and November" and that "militarists and their soldiers have made us their slaves" (December 1924). Ding's father turned 60 this same year, and her busy schedule and the long travel time (30 hours by train) were not the only reasons she chose not to visit: "Trains are loaded with soldiers, and anything might happen to a woman."

The end of the 1920s brought some relief from her duties. First came an invitation to be a delegate at the first Pan-Pacific Women's Conference in Honolulu. "One of the leading international women's social movements of the twentieth century," organizers from the United States, Australia, and New Zealand brought together women from across the globe to promote "inter-cultural exchange" and "inter-racial friendship"

(Paisley 2). Ding at first refused the invitation—Dr. Mary Stone (Shi Meiyu) had also been invited, and Ding "want[ed] Dr. Stone to represent Chinese women doctors" (April 1928). In the end, however, it was Ding who attended the conference and advanced the reputation and independence of China. When Eleanor Hinder, an Australian woman who had worked in Shanghai with the Young Women's Christian Association (YWCA), suggested that the following year's conference be held in Shanghai, Ding rebuffed her. "If the next conference is going to be held in China," Ding said, "the invitation should be from Chinese women." This was "reportedly an electrifying declaration that the time had come when Chinese women would speak for themselves" (Lake 51).

Ding returned to China after the conference only briefly—in 1929, four years after Levi Barbour's death, she was awarded a Barbour Fellowship, a postgraduate research grant at the University of Michigan. Returning to Ann Arbor provided some much-needed time for rest and recovery. During her year-long fellowship, she had the freedom to study as much as she pleased and to attend "good lectures and fine concerts." "I am really having a most joyful time," she wrote once the fall semester had gotten under way (November 1929). Much of her work during the Barbour Fellowship focused on writing a book for mothers in China who needed access to modern obstetric advice. The book was "well received by parents here. Many have expressed that this is just the book they need for care of their children.... Every mother gets a copy before she leaves this hospital" (January 1935). In the book's acknowledgments is a dedication to Levi Barbour and his "foresight and generosity."

Soon after the second printing of Ding's book, the mayor of Tianjin chose Ding to be the director of the Tianjin Infant Asylum, which housed approximately 100 unwanted girls. "This is the first time in the history of Tientsin [Tianjin] to have a woman in a government position," Ding wrote. "The mayor of the city wanted a woman to take this work as he said it is a woman's job" (July 1935). The men, clearly, had not been doing an adequate job:

> *You have no idea what a poor sanitary condition the home was in.... The home had a man doctor who did nothing but took his monthly salary as his side dish. Politics is politics everywhere in the world ... I cannot begin to tell you what sweeping I have done these past two months. I cleared the place of useless men and women who were good for nothing. I actually fired thirty nine people within these two months. (July 1935)*

Ding had come a long way from the nervous graduate forced to take command at the Peiyang Hospital. Here she was comfortably in command. In just the first few months of her leadership, Ding tore down an old, inadequate building and ordered a new one built; organized a class for nursemaids; battled the spread of contagious illness among the residents;

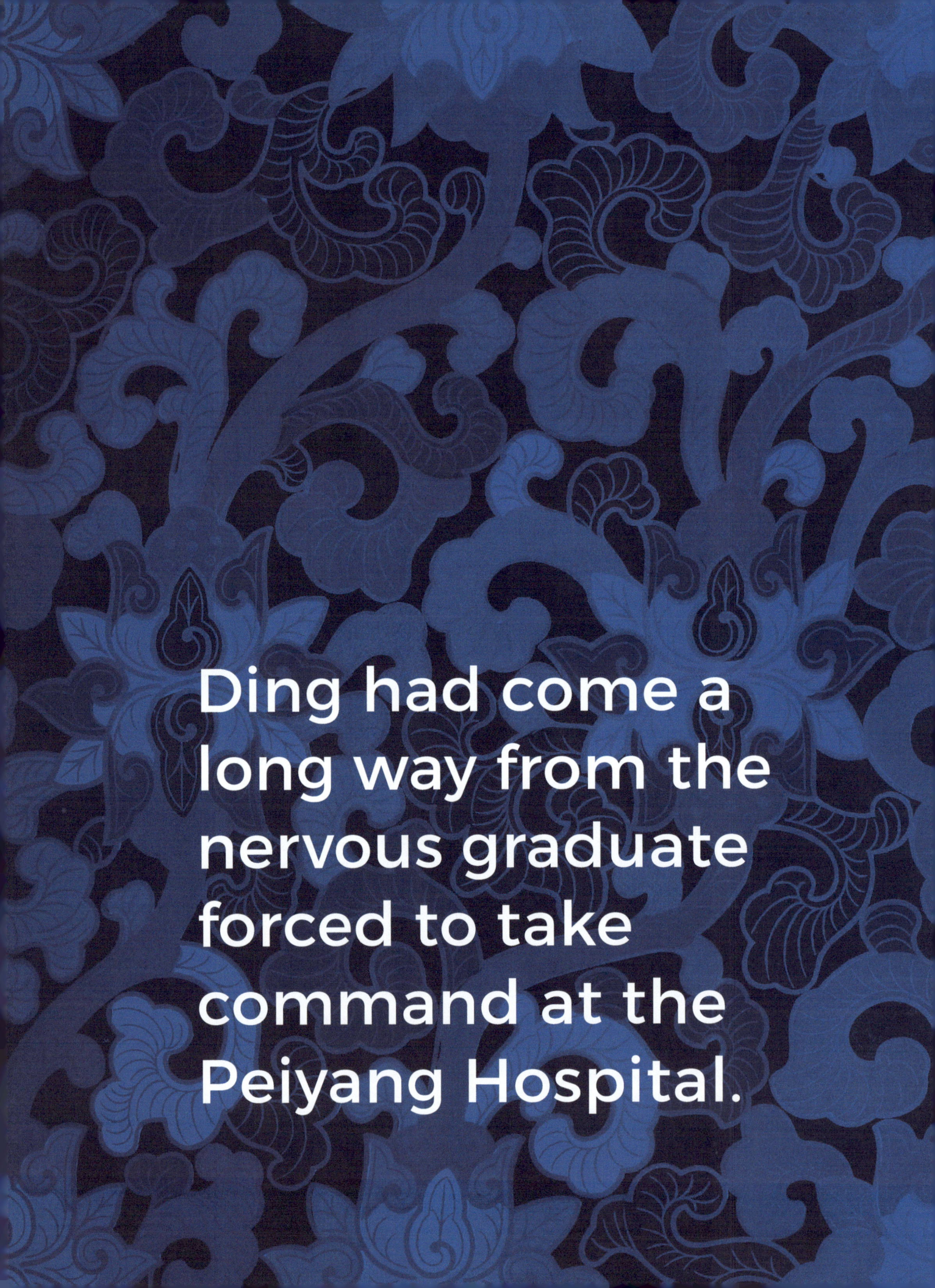

Ding had come a long way from the nervous graduate forced to take command at the Peiyang Hospital.

Ding (center) with her Barbour cohort, 1930. Barbour Scholarship for Oriental Women Committee Records, Bentley Historical Library, University of Michigan.

and devised new diets for the children. She began to teach the older girls to take care of the younger ones: "I am trying to make this institution like a home," she wrote, and one is inclined to believe Ding when she said, "Everybody in the city of Tientsin is happy over the fact that I have been chosen to reorganize this institution" (July 1935).

Despite Ding's pleasure at the progress she was making at the hospital and at the asylum, the threat of armed conflict hovered over all her work and is omnipresent in her letters to Miss Turner. Tianjin in northeastern China had long been a key port, valued by the foreign powers that controlled large concessions in the city for its direct line of sight to the capital, Beijing, little more than 100 kilometers inland. A site of much conflict, the Boxers had seized partial control of Tianjin during the rebellion at the end of the 19th century. Now, as Ding tried to shore up the city's educational and medical infrastructure, the threat from an aggressive Japan loomed over her. Writing at the end of 1935, Ding predicted, "Soon or late Japan will press China into war," before describing being called in for questioning by a Japanese spy (October 1935).

Ding's prediction came true. The Second Sino-Japanese War began in early July 1937, and by the end of the month, Tianjin was under fire. Warplanes bombed some of the city's most important sites, burning Nankai University to the ground and blowing up the police station, which was "very near the hospital" (August 1937). Ding did her best to move her patients, many of whom were "on the point of a nervous breakdown," by ambulance to other locations. Ding herself, however, stayed put, feeling "duty bound" to stay with her hospital (August 1937). Later that year, Ding was able to pass a letter to Miss Turner through an American friend, which meant it was uncensored by the Japanese government. The letter describes further aerial strikes against the city, her hospital being rocked by bombs, and moving patients to the basement: "We are not afraid to die . . . but how long will our nerves last we do not know" (September 1937). Ding addressed Miss Turner in the letter, and through her the rest of the world: "We do not ask the world for anything but a chance to live peacefully by ourselves and harmoniously with others."

After June 1938, there is an eight-month gap between letters. In March 1939, she wrote a letter to Miss Turner that referred to a mutual friend who had informed her of "events here." She followed this up with an ominous line: "I am thankful that as a child I was brought up strictly and simply and accustomed to many small privations" (March 1939). More of the story emerges in later letters—Ding and a nephew were detained for 19 days in prison by the occupying Japanese army. No reason was given for the arrest, though Ding was questioned about her political affiliations: "I won my battle. They could find nothing and they had to give me freedom . . . I am not interested in political affairs at all" (April 1939). A note from Ding's great-niece Evelyn Kay in the Mount Holyoke archive relates an anecdote from Ding's nephew: apparently Ding "persisted on flying the American Flag on her car during the occupation and landed both of them in Japanese Prison."

The Japanese occupation of China continued through the end of World War II. During this time, Ding ministered to thousands of refugees, relocated to Shanghai, gave birth to a baby girl, and survived being buried in rubble by an airstrike. After a year of silence in her correspondence with Miss Turner, Ding described the experience:

> *Soon the buzzing of the heavy bombers and the crackling of the anti-aircrafts were covered up by a series of the whizzing of the descending bombs and the shaking explosions, following one of which I felt myself torn from Ray and thrown into the middle of the room face downward, and the house had come crashing down on me. Instinctively I had thrown up my left arm so that my head came to rest upon it thus leaving a breathing space. The dust was so thick that it was hard to breathe . . . I was not in the least frightened and had wished I were a strong man*

to have the strength to lift up the load on my back so that I could breathe better. The truth was I could not even move a hair. Within half an hour under the guidance of my voice they dug me out without a scratch to speak of, only a large bruise over my left hip bone where I was hit by a beam. . . . Indeed, it was a real good fortune of a misfortune! For there were only six layers of floors and ceilings on top of me; the roof of this room had not caved in nor had the walls fallen. There could have been so many "if's," only one of which could change my year of silence into many years. (June 1941)

Ding spent her postwar years in China working as the chairman of the International Relief Committee. But restoring health and order to Tianjin was not easy; in the wake of the Japanese occupation, the civil war between the Communists and Nationalists reignited. Ding's letters at the end of the 1940s bemoan the loss of rights—freedom of speech, freedom of religion—as the Communists came to power. In her great-niece's recollection, in 1950, Ding left everything behind "when it became apparent that her American education was a danger to her friends" (Ting). She crossed the border into Hong Kong and from there flew to the United Kingdom. Ding sent several letters to Miss Turner from England, writing about the welcome peace and quiet, about her hope that the US Embassy would let her into America, and about her fears for her own country.

In the end, Ding did make it back to America, where she spent two more decades serving as a physician and an instructor. Ding's is a remarkable story. For her, the University of Michigan and the Barbour Fellowship were springboards into a position of authority in China, where she ran hospitals, rebuilt the Tianjin Infant Asylum, chaired the International Relief Committee, and represented her country at international conferences. During some of China's most tumultuous and difficult years, Ding Maoying became a pillar of leadership and support for the cities in which she lived.

Wu Yifang: China's First Female College President

Like Ding Maoying, Wu Yifang studied at the University of Michigan as one of the early Barbour Scholars. She, like Ding, found herself vaulted into a leadership position as a young woman: at 35 years old, having just graduated with an advanced degree in entomology, Wu was selected to be the president of Jinling (Ginling) College in Nanjing, making her the first ever woman in China's history to hold the office. Wu became president at the end of the 1920s, which meant that she was soon to be responsible for keeping the college intact and its students safe during China's civil war and the Japanese invasion. Like Ding Maoying, who was working in the same period in northern China, Wu in the south rose to the occasion in spectacular fashion.

Wu Yifang (center) with two classmates at the University of Michigan. A. Grace Edmonds scrapbooks, Bentley Historical Library, University of Michigan.

Wu Yifang was born in 1893 on the cusp of massive social change in China. As the third of four children in a relatively upper-class family, Wu's feet were bound as a young girl, although they were later unbound. And while her family had once been known for its scholars—her great-grandfather and grandfather had both passed the national civil service examination at the highest ranks—her father had "passed only the lowest level." With her family's fortune dwindling, "Wu's father reluctantly purchased a low-level official job with the help of family connections" (Waelchli 52). Despite the family's financial hardship, Wu Yifang and her older sister, Yifen, managed to get an education. Yifen, in particular, is noted to have been "very much interested" in education. When their parents refused to send them to the new girls' school in Hangzhou, "Yifen, desperate to attend school, attempted suicide." This was enough to persuade their parents, and in the spring of 1904, the two girls, 15 and 11 years old, "took an eleven-day journey by sedan chair, houseboat and steamer to Hangzhou" to attend school (53).

The children had five years to enjoy their education before tragedy struck. In 1909, they received a message calling them home. Their father, it turned out, "had been persuaded to use government finances in two business schemes. When these failed and he was asked to account for the funds, he committed suicide." This began a string of tragedies that shattered the family. Wu Yifang and her sister left school and moved with the rest of the family to Shanghai, where they lived with an uncle. Two years later, Wu's older brother committed suicide as his father had, "drowning himself in the river." Her mother, already ill, died soon after. And on the night of her mother's funeral, Wu's older sister, faced with the overwhelming task of caring for her siblings alone, committed suicide herself. Wu, now just 18 years old, had "lost her three closest relatives within a month" (Waelchli 55).

In the years that followed, Wu Yifang leaned on her uncle, Chen Shutong, who encouraged her to continue her education. In fact, "according to one of Wu's former students who knew her well," Wu Yifang also "contemplated suicide after the deaths of her family members," and it was partly due to her uncle's support and encouragement that she survived her grief (Waelchli 56). In the winter of 1916, Wu enrolled in the recently opened Jinling College, and it was there that she truly began to recover from her family's dissolution. As Wu remarked in a tribute to a friend, Zee Yuh-tsung,

> *When I entered Jinling, I had suffered deep sorrow from a family tragedy. . . . In Jinling it was Yuh-tsung's Christian Life and her loving sympathy for me that uplifted me out of self-imposed isolation. Gradually I understood the real meaning of life and learned to aim at a worthy life purpose. (57)*

As a college student, Wu Yifang displayed a natural bent toward leadership. She organized a student government association in which she served as chairwoman and then president of her senior class; she also "push[ed] for more student autonomy," intent on showing "that students were capable of enforcing dormitory rules and other regulations themselves" (Waelchli 58). But perhaps even more important, the students at Jinling College imagined for themselves a position of agency in China more generally. In a class skit, Wu Yifang played an upper-class lady who decided to give gifts to the poor instead of her wealthy friends; in another skit, the four class presidents "gave a presentation depicting Jinling women as a light going out to China." The college students were not shy about putting these ideals into practice, opening a "half-day school for illiterate girls" and starting a "Sunday school for neighborhood children" (60).

Upon graduating from Jinling with a bachelor's degree, Wu Yifang applied for and received a Barbour Scholarship at the University of Michigan. For the next six years, she worked through master's and PhD programs in entomology, teaching classes to undergraduates and continuing her own research as a graduate student. But in 1927, before Wu had even finished her doctorate program, she received word that the Jinling College Committee (GCC), a governing board made up of representatives from American missionaries and colleges, had elected her to be Jinling's next president. She would be the first Chinese woman to ever hold such a post—the position was hers, if she wanted it.

While Wu had made a name for herself as both a diligent scholar and a willing leader, electing someone not yet out of a doctorate program with no administrative experience was still an unorthodox decision. And in fact, the GCC would not have made such a

Wu Yifang (top row, fourth from left) with her Barbour cohort, 1925. Barbour Scholarship for Oriental Women Committee Records, Bentley Historical Library, University of Michigan.

Wu Yifang with Mrs. George Nichols. Anne Louise Welch Papers, Bentley Historical Library, University of Michigan.

decision if not for pressure from the Nationalist government to place Chinese citizens at high levels of Western-run institutions. Antiforeign and anti-imperialist sentiment came to a head during the "Nanjing Incident," in which several Western men, including the vice president of the University of Nanjing, were killed by roving bands of southern soldiers. When one such mob came to Jinling's campus with "slogans like 'Kill the Foreigners,'" Jinling's foreign faculty hid in an attic while the Chinese faculty led the soldiers on a "wild goose chase around the buildings" (Waelchli 100). While Jinling's foreign faculty managed to flee Nanjing safely, this proved to be a turning point in the college's administration, even when the faculty eventually returned to the city. After the violence died down, it became clear that Chiang Kai-shek's Kuomintang government meant to enforce the regulation about Chinese leadership in local institutions, and the GCC got down to the business of electing a Chinese president.

For Wu herself, though, the decision to accept the position was a difficult one. While Wu had planned to return to Jinling as a professor of biology, accepting the leadership of the whole institution was a much more fearsome proposition. Writing to a member of the GCC, Wu said,

> *I learned of the possibility of being called to fill an important position during this transition period, and I had to face the fact that I am not the least bit prepared for such a task. I never expected to go into administrative work and always wanted to teach along my own line of Biology. I thought over the situation carefully and told Mrs. New frankly that even if circumstances should turn out to be such that I ought—duty toward Jinling—to accept the position, it will be just temporary, only for this sudden and short period of transition. If conditions should become such that no great change is necessary, or if the Board of Control should succeed in finding some other person for the position, I would be only too glad to serve G.C. as a teaching faculty. (Waelchli 111–112)*

Despite Wu Yifang's misgivings, she returned to China in the summer of 1928 and seemed to fall naturally into the role of Jinling College's president. That autumn, she gave an inauguration speech that was "beautiful and moving" and filled the students with pride in their "young, pretty president." Her first months reassured the GCC that they had made a good decision: "More and more I am coming to have respect for and confidence in her judgment and ability . . . I think she has already won the confidence of her faculty." The former president of Jinling, Matilda Thurston, who had been unceremoniously ousted from her position, wrote that because of Wu Yifang's capability, "my heart is at rest about Jinling" (Waelchli 119).

Wu earned the confidence and satisfaction of Jinling's old guard by resolving a crisis that arose "less than a month" into her tenure: "A general wanted to commandeer the campus as temporary headquarters for Shanxi warlord Yan Xishan" (Waelchli 120–121). Luckily, Wu was able to use political contacts to resolve the situation, asking an old school friend's husband to make an appeal to the foreign minister (121).

For the next decade, Wu Yifang became an increasingly public figure, both internationally and at home in China. Almost as soon as she was elected, Wu began to be asked to speak at conferences. In 1929, she traveled to Japan as a delegate at the Institute of Pacific Relations; four years later, she represented China at the International Women's Congress in Chicago, and while in America, she "visited thirty-three cities and spoke over two hundred times" (Waelchli 139). Wu joined and led several Christian associations in China, including the National Christian Council, which elected her as chairwoman in 1935. In just a few short years, Wu had gone from studying biology as a graduate student at the University of Michigan to being one of the most famous women in China: "By the early 1940s, she was so well known by certain groups in America that she was sometimes referred to as the second most important woman in China, behind Soong Mei-ling," wife of Chiang Kai-shek, head of the Nationalist government (138).

In fact, despite Jinling's troubles with Nationalist troops and some early "misgivings" on Wu's part about Chiang Kai-shek's leadership, by the 1930s, Wu Yifang "supported Chiang and became good friends with his wife, Soong Mei-ling." Wu began to receive social invitations from the Chiangs, and at several national conferences and dinners, they were seated together. In the winter of 1934, Jinling College invited Chiang and his wife to a "baccalaureate service," where the generalissimo "gave a short talk." In 1936, Zhang Xueliang, "the Young Marshall"—a military ally and confidant of Chiang Kai-shek—betrayed Chiang, kidnapping him to be used as a bargaining chip with the increasingly powerful Communist Party. Wu, hearing the news, "went immediately to see Soong Mei-ling." Jinling canceled its holiday plans, and Wu is said to have taken Chiang's kidnapping "so personally that it was almost impossible to carry on her work"; when "Chiang was released, Wu personally informed the faculty and students" (Waelchli 143).

Wu Yifang's position as the president of Jinling College—one of the only accredited colleges for women in China and the only woman to hold such an office—placed her squarely on the national and international stage. And although she came to the position with little formal leadership experience, Wu seems to have inhabited her new role with grace and ease, charming even the highest levels of China's leadership. However, the Second Sino-Japanese War (1937–1945) was perhaps the greatest test of Wu Yifang's capacity for leadership. As the Japanese army pushed through China's northeastern coast and prepared to invade southern China, Wu dedicated herself to guiding her college and her country through the conflict. Wu ran the Chinese Women's Association for War Relief alongside Soong Mei-ling, contributed to a Christian organization for war relief, comforted and guided her students through the first air raids over Nanjing, and advised her foreign faculty on whether to leave the city. All in all, she was, as a colleague described her, a "great and fearless general" and "solid rock through and through" (Waelchli 172–173).

As the war escalated, however, the government ordered universities in the Nanjing area to close. Jinling shut down all classes and dismissed the faculty and staff except for a skeleton crew of an "emergency committee" and opened several smaller provisional branches farther inland. Some of Jinling's Western faculty, against the advice of the consulate, remained in Nanjing and "deflected requests for use of the buildings to keep them in reserve for civilian relief efforts" (Waelchli 171). By the end of the first year of the war, the invasion of Nanjing was all but imminent, and Wu's colleagues and the GCC begged her to leave the city. That December, Wu gave in, boarding a British vessel due to leave Nanjing: "Wu had gotten out of Nanjing just in time; shipping on that part of the Yangtse river came to a halt shortly thereafter" (175).

Leaving her college and her colleagues alone in a city under fire felt to Wu like running away, even though she continued to manage Jinling from a provisional outpost in Wuchang. As Wu sailed away from her all-but-fallen city, she was struck by a deep sense of guilt—as she called it, "the most agonizing experience I had. . . . On the boat I did not have any peace, thinking of the small committee I left behind to take charge, and thinking of all the large number of people who could not get away" (Waelchli 174). No sooner had Wu set sail than she reconsidered her decision to close the school. Perhaps, as she wrote in transit, it was up to her to "follow the hard course . . . I for one am ready to go if and when the college is to start work" (175).

It is a good thing that Wu was unable to turn back: she set sail on one of the last barges out of the city on December 1. Eleven days later, on December 12, "General Tang Shengzhi, charged with defending the city, abruptly left Nanjing" (Waelchli 176). In the days that followed, Japanese soldiers poured into the city, "engaging in an orgy of violence including rape, looting, arson, and killing" now known as the Rape of Nanking. As this trauma unfolded, Jinling College became a refuge for hundreds, then thousands of women and children fleeing the terror in the rest of the city. The emergency committee hung American flags on the walls of the campus in an effort to deter Japanese soldiers, and when that didn't work, one woman, Minnie Vautrin, ran across the campus challenging marauding soldiers, doing her best to be a shield for the refugees within.

In the later days of the war, Wu Yifang led Jinling College from its new home in the city of Chengdu. There was an unending list of practical problems to solve: attracting qualified students, finding new faculty, funding the school, and supplying students with food as prices surged. And yet Wu still found time to continue her larger political efforts. In addition to her war relief work, Wu was elected to the Kuomintang's parliamentary body, the People's Political Council (PPC), where she eventually was chosen to belong to the five-person presidium that also included Generalissimo Chiang (Waelchli 233). Not only was she 1 of only 10 women in the whole 200-person PPC; she was the only woman on the elite presidium. Just as she had quickly won over the faculty of Jinling as a new president, Wu Yifang was soon recognized as one of the most valuable members of the presidium: "Local newspapers deemed her the best presiding officer . . . Capable [and] hard working, . . . [she] dealt with motions in a closely reasoned and well-argued fashion" (233–234).

As a cap on an already remarkable career, in 1945, Wu was chosen to be one of the nine Chinese delegates (again the only woman) sent to the San Francisco Conference to establish the United Nations charter. Despite health troubles and mounting work at Jinling, Wu accepted the offer. She saw China's position among the UN's permanent members, the "Big Five" nations, as another step along the road toward a unified country and a representative government. In the face of continued conflict between the Chinese Communist Party and the Nationalist government, Wu saw that China had more work yet to do:

> *China as one of the "Five" must build up herself [and] develop a strong democracy and industrialize in order to support our moral stand on respecting international law and justice. I see a great future for our country, but it depends upon how our government and people will respond. (Waelchli 251)*

Wu Yifang spent the rest of her life helping China do this work. She ran Jinling College through the end of China's civil war; through the reconstruction of the campus in Nanjing; through the country's transition to Communism and concerns about political reprisals; through the growing anti-American sentiment that threatened Jinling's foreign faculty and, by 1951, forced them to resign en masse; and through Jinling's eventual merger with the University of Nanjing.

Beloved by her students and colleagues and by local and national politicians, and with few critics recorded anywhere, Wu Yifang seems to have been an ideal leader. She worked only for the well-being of her students and fellow citizens; for example, she voluntarily turned over extra income from speaking engagements to Jinling College. Wu had the gift of seeing the best in any situation, of working flexibly in many political contexts. And yet, somehow, Wu Yifang never lost her critical edge: over the years, she spoke and wrote critically of any policy—American, Nationalist, or Communist—that seemed likely to be harmful to her beloved college and country.

Wu Yifang (third from right) with the Chinese delegation (including T. V. Soong, center) at the UN summit in San Francisco, 1945. Courtesy of United Nations Photo Library.

Wu Yifang addresses a crowd at a dedication of a Chinese aircraft during the San Francisco UN summit, 1945. Courtesy of United Nations Photo Library.

Barbour's Legacy

It is a testament to Levi Barbour's generosity and foresight—and to the large number of ambitious, brilliant Chinese women who sought an education during an era when doing so was far outside the norm—that there are far more worthy Barbour Scholars to discuss than can possibly fit in one chapter or one book. Wu and Ding are just two of hundreds of noteworthy Barbour Scholars, including Lucy Wang, who became president of Hwa Nan College soon after Wu was elected at Jinling, or the famous playwright Li Man-Kuei. The accomplishments of the Barbour Scholars are so great that they deserve a book unto themselves.

Portrait of Lucy Wang (left) with two other Barbour Scholars. Barbour Scholarship for Oriental Women Committee Records, Bentley Historical Library, University of Michigan.

Works Cited

Barbour, Levi L. *College Training for Professional Men.* Lansing, MI: R. Smith, 1897. Print.

Barry, Sara, and Jennifer Grow. "To Boldly Go." *Alumnae Quarterly*, Spring 2015. Web. <http://alumnae.mtholyoke.edu/blog/to-boldly-go/>.

Bordin, Ruth B. "Levi Lewis Barbour: Benefactor of University of Michigan Women." *Michigan Quarterly Review* 2 (1963): 36. Print.

Ding, Maoying. "Letters to Abby Turner, 1915–1950." Me-Iung Ding Letters. Web. 15 Nov. 2016. <https://www.mtholyoke.edu/~dalbino/letters/mting.html>.

Faerber, Karen Irene. "The Levi L. Barbour Scholarship for Asian Women." Master's thesis, Eastern Michigan U, 16 Nov. 1994. Print.

Lake, Marilyn. "The ILO, Australia, and the Asia-Pacific Region." *The ILO from Geneva to the Pacific Rim: West Meets East.* Ed. Jill Jensen. London: Palgrave Macmillan, 2016. Print.

Paisley, Fiona. *Glamour in the Pacific: Cultural Internationalism and Race Politics in the Women's Pan-Pacific.* Honolulu: U of Hawaii P, 2009. Print.

Semenza, Nevada. "China's Great Need for Women Leadership Finds Its Answer in the Halls of Jinling, Cathay's Edition of America's Smith College." *China Press*, 22 July 1931. Print.

Ting, Evelyn Kay. "Me-Iung Ting x1916." Web. 15 Nov. 2016. <https://www.mtholyoke.edu/~dalbino/letters/women/mting.html>.

Waelchli, Mary Jo. "Abundant Life: Matilda Thurston, Wu Yifang and Jinling College, 1915–1951." Order no. 3059344, Ohio State U, 2002. Print.

Xiong, Rosalinda. *Jinling College, the University of Michigan and the Barbour Scholarship.* Singapore: Rosalinda Xiong, 2016. Print.

5
Turn-of-the-Century Intellectuals

Despite China's multimillennial history of intellectual achievement, at the end of the 19th century, China was still emerging from the Qing dynasty's period of scientific stagnation. As the Opium Wars in the mid-1800s and the disastrous treaties that followed made clear, without an industrial revolution of their own, China had unwittingly fallen behind in the technological race. Despite efforts at reform and a push for "self-strengthening," the Qing dynasty was ultimately unable to catch up.

The Republican period that followed, however, began to change all that. Within a few decades, China inaugurated some of its most prestigious universities: Peking University in 1898, Tsinghua in 1911, and the Academia Sinica in 1928. During these years, young Chinese intellectuals often studied abroad at foreign institutions and brought their new expertise home to help nurture fledgling academic disciplines. Several graduates of the University of Michigan (U-M) did exactly this. Zheng Zuoxin (Cheng Tso-Hsin) studied at U-M and went on to become the premier ornithologist in China, the man who wrote the definitive textbooks and began China's ornithological tradition. Wu Dayou (Wu Ta-You) was one of the first three men in China to earn a degree in theoretical physics and is often cited as the "father of Chinese physics." And John C. H. Wu (Wu Jingxiong), a legal scholar and philosopher who befriended some of the most important thinkers of the day, was the principal architect of the constitution of the Republic of China.

All three men, graduates of the University of Michigan, helped define and advance their disciplines. The seeds of China's current scientific and intellectual prominence can be found in scholars like them.

Zheng Zuoxin: Father of Ornithology in China

Born in 1906, Zheng Zuoxin's devotion to and fascination with the natural world began as a small child. Zheng's mother passed away when he was only eight years old, leaving him to be raised primarily by his grandmother. They lived in the port city of Fuzhou, where half a century earlier, Judson Collins had arrived as a missionary. Fuzhou sits where the Minjiang and Wulong Rivers run down to meet the sea, and in one anecdote, Zheng's grandmother sent him out to the riverbank to catch crabs for dinner. When he brought back more than enough to eat, "the surplus to those requirements went into his aquarium for study" (Rank).

Having learned some English from his father and uncle, both scholars, 15-year-old Zheng entered Fujian (Fukien) Christian University, where he continued to study biology. Zheng graduated in 1926 and, "encouraged by a cousin who worked in a Michigan car plant," enrolled as a graduate student in the University of Michigan's zoology program (Rank). And although Zheng had grown up interested in birds (he told stories about how, as a child in Fujian, he would "come across the crested ibis, now one of the world's rarest birds"; another anecdote describes Zheng learning to identify birds by their calls as early as primary school), it wasn't until late in his education that he identified ornithology as his chosen discipline (Rank; Hsu, "In Memoriam" 540). In fact, Zheng devoted his doctoral research to embryology, writing articles on the intersexuality of frogs.

Zheng had already received his PhD when he was inspired to switch disciplines. In the summer of 1930, just after Zheng's graduation, he visited one of the University of Michigan's museums,

Zheng Zuoxin at the Institute of Zoology in Beijing, 1978. Courtesy of the American Ornithological Society.

where he came across a "specimen of the golden pheasant (most likely Chrysolophus pictus)—a bird with strikingly colorful feathers native to China. [Zh]eng was stunned by its beauty, but more shocked by the fact that birds endemic to China had to be studied and named by foreigners. He decided to switch the focus of his career to studying birds in China" (Gao).

The next 20 years of Zheng Zuoxin's career are a laundry list of accomplishments. Arriving back home in China in 1930, Zheng immediately found work at his alma mater, Fukien Christian University (FCU), as "Professor and Director of the Department of Biology" (Hsu, "In Memoriam" 540). Four years later, he helped found the China Zoological Society, an organization that today continues to promote scientific exchange, publish research, and educate youth. And when FCU was forced to evacuate inland during the Japanese invasion of World War II, Zheng was still able to make the best of the situation, publishing articles on the birds of the region and organizing research expeditions into the Wuyi Mountains nearby (Gao). As the war came to a close, Zheng Zuoxin was invited to the United States as a visiting professor, and on his return to FCU, "he became Dean of Science and Dean of both Undergraduate and Graduate studies" (Hsu, "In Memoriam" 540). The publication of his *Checklist of Chinese Birds*, the first of its kind in Chinese, followed soon after. By 1950, Zheng had moved to Beijing, where he came into his own as a father of the ornithological tradition in China. In three years, he became the lead ornithological curator for the Academia Sinica's Institute of Zoology, founded the Peking Natural History Museum, and was chosen to be the director of the Ornithological Department at the Chinese Academy of Sciences.

The end of the 1950s brought a period of difficulty for Zheng Zuoxin. The year 1958 marked the beginning of Chairman Mao Zedong's "Great Leap Forward" initiative to rapidly mobilize and industrialize the country. One now notorious part of this movement was a hygiene campaign in which the government exhorted citizens to get rid of the "Four Pests": rats, flies, mosquitoes, and sparrows. Although not disease vectors like the other three, sparrows were targeted because they ate grain in the fields that would have otherwise gone to hungry citizens. The masses were encouraged to kill sparrows whenever possible, to break their eggs, and to bang pots and pans to prevent them from landing and resting. In the end, this campaign had the opposite effect— as the sparrow population plummeted, the locust population skyrocketed, contributing to the Great Famine that followed the Great Leap.

As an ornithologist, Zheng Zuoxin must have seen the errors of the "Four Pest" campaign before the consequences became clear. As one obituary put it, he "did his best to oppose" the campaign, despite his lack of political influence. In an interview in 1979, Zheng played down his role:

> *In the period after the Liberation and after the mass movement against the four "pests," Chairman Mao pointed out that sparrows needed to be studied with respect to the harm they did as well as their benefit to orchards and farms. Ornithologists now have returned to basic problems. (Grimm and Zheng 106)*

Zheng Zuoxin's expertise and life work clashed again with the government during the Cultural Revolution in the late 1960s and early 1970s. With the demonization of the "Four Olds" (old customs, ideas, habits, and culture) came a backlash against the intellectual elite of China. Zheng was one of the many forced into manual labor, "imprisoned in a cowshed and made to sweep courtyards and clean lavatories" (Rank). In the aforementioned 1979 interview, however, Zheng described how even despite these conditions, he was able to keep working:

> *Some professors were sent to the countryside to work while others were able to continue their work. I was one of them, spending much of my time revising a textbook on vertebrate taxonomy and undertaking some ornithological investigations. Much of the scientific work, however, stopped, and the work of various societies stopped. (Grimm and Zheng 108)*

After the trials of the Cultural Revolution, Zheng Zuoxin resumed in earnest the work that he loved. He published a number of volumes of research and reference material, including the enormous *A Synopsis of the Avifauna of China*. He performed ecological conservation work with the Chinese Academy of Sciences, which chose him to be the lead delegate at international conferences and for negotiations with Japan.

Zheng Zuoxin passed away in 1998 at the age of 92 as a legend in his field. All modern Chinese ornithology has been built on the foundation left behind by Zheng Zuoxin's lifetime of devotion to the birds and wildlife of China.

Wu Dayou: Father of Chinese Physics

Wu Dayou spent his early childhood traveling between northern and southern China, between the humid, subtropical city of Guangzhou just northwest of Hong Kong and the northern port city of Tianjin. His was a family of scholars: Wu's grandfather had attained "the highest degree in the imperial examination system, and had won election to the Imperial Hanlin Academy in Peking," while Wu's father had achieved the second-highest degree. In Imperial China, such scholarly achievement opened doors to a life of civil service. Wu's father worked for the government, first as a diplomat at the "Chinese embassy in the Philippines" and later as a magistrate of a county in Manchuria ("Wu Ta-you: Biography"). Wu and his mother followed his father north, stopping short of Manchuria and settling in Tianjin. But when his father died of a plague illness soon after taking office, Wu and his mother spent a decade moving among different groups of extended family.

Despite his father's early passing and the dislocation that followed, Wu Dayou was ultimately able to carry on his family's history of scholarly achievement. And although his legacy is now cemented as one of the men who would "lead China to modern physics," as a young man entering Nankai University in Tianjin, Wu in fact "never planned to be a physicist" (Hsu, "Scientific Research" 1). As a freshman, he enrolled in the Mining Department because, he said, the job prospects

Wu as a young child. Courtesy of the Wu Memorial Lectures at the University at Buffalo.

looked better. More telling, perhaps, is Wu's perception that because "his ability to understand and analyze was better than his creativity," mining would be a better fit. Luckily, he was given a chance to prove himself when the mining school closed due to lack of funding. Wu transferred to the Department of Physics, and although he passed all his classes, it wasn't until his sophomore year that a lecture on modern physics by Yao Yu-Tai sparked a "prairie fire" of curiosity (2).

Even with all this new enthusiasm, however, on graduating, Wu failed to receive Tsinghua University's scholarship to study abroad. He spent the next five years teaching at Nankai University and continuing his education in private. He read works by physicists such as Arnold Sommerfeld and Max Planck in his spare time, translated texts into Chinese, and organized a "Seminar Club" with senior students to study and discuss high-level physics (Hsu, "Scientific Research" 2). In 1931, Wu applied again for a research scholarship, and this time he was successful. With funding from the China

Foundation for the Promotion of Education and Culture, Wu enrolled in the Physics Department at the University of Michigan.

The University of Michigan is where Wu came into his own as a scientist and a researcher. Many decades later, during a symposium in his honor at U-M, Wu could still recall the fall day of his arrival in Ann Arbor and the exact classes he took during his first semester. As one might expect from a student thirsty for knowledge and absorbed in the possibilities of his work, most of the recollections in Wu's talk were about his research, his mentors, his breakthroughs. And although his thesis paper apparently did not garner much attention from the scientific community when it was published, it has since been recognized as ahead of its time, "the pioneering work in the study of transuranium elements, long before they were actually discovered by Glenn T. Seaborg" (Hsu, "Scientific Research" 3). Wu himself described his time at the University of Michigan with charm and humility, saying, "You can see that I had the best opportunities for a good start in physics; only my ability was not equal to my opportunities" (Wu, "Reminiscences" 26).

This, however, is patently untrue—his ability exceeded even his opportunities. Wu graduated from the University of Michigan in record time, receiving his doctorate in 1933, just two years after enrolling as a graduate student. A year later, Wu returned to China, where the prestigious Peking University hired him to their physics faculty alongside Wu's old mentor Yao Yu-Tai. Wu brought experimental research experience, cutting-edge curiosity, and "the radically new physics" to both his department and China as a whole (Hsu, "Scientific Research" 4). Even as the threat of wartime loomed, in the three years between Wu's return and the start of the Second Sino-Japanese War, he was incredibly productive, publishing "15 papers in physics journals in the US, England, and China" in addition to his teaching duties and collaborations with other faculty (5).

The Japanese invasion threatened to halt all progress. The initial brunt of the attack was borne by Tianjin, Wu's childhood home and a port city only a short distance away from Beijing. Tianjin fell to Japanese forces in the summer of 1937 soon after fighting began, and with the gateway to the

Wu with theoretical physicist Paul Dirac. Courtesy of the Wu Memorial Lectures at the University at Buffalo.

country thrown open, Beijing soon followed. In winter 1937, the presidents of several of China's largest universities—Tsinghua, Peking, and Nankai—"joined forces to establish a temporary university in exile." They moved inland to Kunming, Yunnan, and became the "National Southwest Associated University" (Hsu, "Scientific Research" 6).

Wu survived this wartime dislocation just as he had survived his childhood relocations between northern and southern China. And yet, times were tough. His wife, a sweetheart from his years at Nankai University, grew gravely ill during this period (Hsu, "Scientific Research" 8). Wu became the sole caretaker, shopping at the market and cooking over a charcoal fire, always worried about rising inflation and the cost of food during wartime. Still, despite these heavy concerns and a lack of institutional resources, Wu made progress in his field. He wrote and published *Vibrational Spectra and Structure of Polyatomic Molecules*, a "ground-breaking book" and the "only book of the subject at that time" (6). And when the joint university "could not afford laboratory space for its faculty members to conduct experimental research," Wu's relentless intellectual drive led him to construct a makeshift lab in a room of his own house.

It was during this time that Wu's skills as a teacher and mentor came into their own. Many students under his guidance went on to extraordinary accomplishments. The two most famous, perhaps, are Yang Chen Ning (C. N. Yang) and Lee Tsung-Dao (T. D. Lee). Yang was a graduate student who "finished his thesis . . . under Prof. Wu's guidance," while Lee, as a young man, a "chubby teenaged boy," came to Wu for help in 1945 (Hsu, "Scientific Research" 8). A gifted and precocious student, Lee wanted Wu's assistance in transferring to the National Southwest Associated University. Wu persuaded the school to allow Lee to sit in on several classes—if he could pass the end-of-term examinations, he would be admitted. Lee, of course, passed the classes easily. What's more, he

> *came to see Wu every day and asked for more books, articles, and homework problems. . . . Sometimes, Prof. Wu would give him difficult books to read and difficult problems to do to stop him from coming every day. Yet, no matter how difficult they were, Lee would always finish them quickly and come back to ask for more! (8)*

In 1957, Lee and Yang were awarded the Nobel Prize for their collaborations. On hearing that he was to receive the award, Yang wrote a letter to his old mentor expressing "deep gratitude" and saying that his work "is traceable directly or indirectly to the ideas I learned from you that Spring fifteen years ago."

With the end of World War II, the civil war in China between Chiang Kai-shek's Nationalist forces and the Communist Party began in earnest. Conditions in Beijing were still complicated; "it was a very difficult time for universities and the professors associated with them" (Hsu, "Scientific Research" 9). Rather than return to Beijing, Wu accepted an invitation from the University of Michigan to return as a visiting professor.

Wu in 1997 with his protégés and Nobel Prize winners C. N. Yang (left) and T. D. Lee (right). Courtesy of the Wu Memorial Lectures at the University at Buffalo.

Wu with his former student and Nobel Prize winner T. D. Lee. Courtesy of the Wu Memorial Lectures at the University at Buffalo.

From Ann Arbor, he traveled to New York, joining the faculty of Columbia University, and then in 1949 moved again to Canada at the invitation of the National Research Council, which hoped that he would chair a theoretical physics group. So began a long period of work "without interruptions" as Wu lived in Canada until 1963 and then took a position at the State University of New York in Buffalo.

Spending the latter half of his career working at Western institutions meant that Wu avoided the turmoil brewing in the early years of the People's Republic, from the Communist victory over the Nationalists to the Great Leap Forward and the Cultural Revolution. However, Wu remained intensely invested in the state of science in China, and he found that he was best able to contribute in Taiwan, home of the exiled Kuomintang government after 1949. Here he spent several summers, teaching

Wu Dayou with US president George H. W. Bush and First Lady Barbara Bush. Courtesy of the Wu Memorial Lectures at the University at Buffalo.

and lecturing on the invitation of the Academia Sinica, before moving permanently to Taipei. The final decades of Wu's life were aimed at the single goal of advancing science and science education. He helped found the National Science Council in Taiwan, serving for several years as its minister; he wrote several seminal Chinese textbooks on theoretical physics; on behalf of the Ministry of Education, he embarked "upon a complete review and reorganization of the science curricula of junior and senior high schools"; and he served as the president of the Academia Sinica, where he implemented a "tenure system to increase research productivity and demand accountability," paving the way for the modernization of that institution ("Wu Ta-you: Biography"; Chun 583).

A portrait of Wu Dayou. Courtesy of the Wu Memorial Lectures at the University at Buffalo.

The effect of Wu Dayou's creativity and enthusiasm as both a scientist and a leader remains crystal clear to his students, his colleagues, and the generations of Chinese scientists who succeed him. As a former student of his, J. P. Hsu writes,

More than any other individual, Wu Dayou is credited for raising physics to its current level in both mainland China and Taiwan. . . . It seems fair to say that Taiwan's scientific and technological development today is to a large part the result of his effort. (Hsu, "Scientific Research" 11)

John C. H. Wu: Legal Scholar, Theologian, and Architect of the Republic of China's Constitution

John C. H. Wu (Wu Jingxiong) was an intellectual omnivore who studied at universities across the globe, initiated lifelong friendships with both US Supreme Court Justice Oliver Wendell Holmes and theologian Thomas Merton, and translated Chinese poetry and philosophy into English in addition to many of his own books and essays on legal philosophy and jurisprudence. But perhaps Wu's most significant contribution was to help mold China's legal system as a chief justice of a provisional court in Shanghai and as one of the primary authors of the Republic of China's constitution.

Wu was born at exactly the time when China most needed an individual of his capacities to help define and defend her independence. He was born in 1899, the year of the Boxer Rebellion's violent rejection of the Western powers that had been making legal, cultural, and financial inroads into China's sovereignty. The rebellion was eventually

The effect of Wu Dayou's creativity and enthusiasm as both a scientist and a leader remains crystal clear to his students, his colleagues, and the generations of Chinese scientists who succeed him.

thwarted, but less by the Chinese government than "by the military interventions of eight Western countries. As a result, China opened its doors to the Western world... not just the trade system but the entire judicial and political system" (Zhang 199). Western countries cemented their footholds in port cities like Shanghai by first gaining administrative control over their concessions within the city and then establishing legal authority with independent court systems that had jurisdiction over their foreign citizens.

Chinese legal scholars resisted this erosion of independence: "For example, in 1912, the Shanghai Bar Association ('SBA') was created by a group of twelve Chinese lawyers who were 'indignant that the foreign concessions have extraterritoriality, while our own nation's independence is incomplete'" (Zhang 200). In a little more than a decade, a Western-educated Wu would arrive in Shanghai to help China reclaim its independence and establish a modern legal tradition.

John C. H. Wu's autobiography, *Beyond East and West*, gives us a sense of his early life in colorful detail. He was born in the city of Ningpo, just across the bay from Shanghai, in the spring of 1899. In that preindustrial era, he wrote, the city was full of vigor and wonder:

> *The sun, the moon, the stars, the winds and rains, the dogs and cats, the birds and flowers, seem to be more human in Ningpo than anywhere else.... A Ningponese enjoys the gift of life as a hungry school boy in America would enjoy a hot dog. (Wu Beyond East, 14)*

He was born into a large family, with both a birth ("little") mother and a "big" mother, who was his father's first and primary wife: "Nobody is perfect, and my big mother had her faults, the chief of which was jealousy of my little mother. She wanted the children but did not like the mother" (Wu 35). Despite this tension, Wu felt deeply connected to his big mother: "I have dreamed of her more often than of any other person. I have wept more tears in memory of her than of anyone else" (33). Wu's little mother passed away when he was only 4, and his father when he was 10. "I have not seen such a beautiful death in my life," Wu wrote of his father's passing.

> *On his death bed, he seemed to be in ecstasy during several hours, casting glances from time to time at the windows and saying constantly, "Behold, eight busa (gods or angels) to conduct me to heaven! What a condescension! How unworthy I am of it!" (24)*

The death of Wu's big mother five years later was not so peaceful. Wu, 15, had been stricken with typhoid fever; he woke one morning to find that the stress and exhaustion of caring for him had caused a blood vessel to rupture in his mother's brain: "She sacrificed her life in saving me from death.... For several months after, I was almost out of my senses" (Wu Beyond East, 37).

In dealing with his grief, Wu threw himself into his schooling. He studied first at the Hsiao Shih Junior College, where he found himself fascinated by physics and the natural sciences until, he wrote, a chemistry accident brought his enthusiasm to a halt:

> *I wanted to see how the hydrogen would burn in the bottle. I tried to light it with a match, but immediately the bottle burst to pieces. Somehow I did not get hurt... and began to wonder if a peeping Tom like myself who could not control his whimsical curiosity was fit to handle the elements. (Wu Beyond East, 56)*

The study of law, however, quickly replaced the sciences: "My heart leaped on hearing the word 'law.' To my mind, law was the science of society just as science was the law of nature" (56). Wu enrolled in the Law School of Peiyang University in Tianjin in 1916 and then transferred to the Comparative Law School of China in Shanghai in 1917.

Wu's three years at the Comparative Law School shaped and prefigured the rest of his career. It was at this school that he learned to speak English fluently, that he converted to Christianity, and that he decided to attend the University of Michigan Law School—the dean of the Comparative Law School in 1920, the year Wu graduated, was himself a graduate of the U-M Law School. In the autumn of 1920, Wu set sail for the United States. His religious faith reached an early peak of intensity. As a "zealous Christian," he would "sneak out from my cabin when my roommates were fast asleep to the stern of the ship, where I would pray on my knees for an hour or so" (Wu 75). On reaching America, however, Wu found himself both increasingly absorbed by his worldly studies and disillusioned with the promise of the United States as a "Christian nation":

> *By imperceptible degrees my interest and faith in Christianity waned. I ceased to pray and go to church ... I was scandalized at hearing my American schoolmates swear in the most irreverent manner by the name of Christ. In the janitor's quarters they were wishing one another to become millionaires in the future ... I found to my great surprise that the almighty dollar was America's God! (76)*

In the place of faith, Wu threw himself into his studies as he had after the death of his parents. He was, by all accounts, a gifted student. His instructors "took a personal interest" in him, including one Professor Drake, who called Wu "a prodigy." Wu himself certainly felt at home at the University: "There was a certain homelikeness and coziness about Ann Arbor, and a warm sympathy about its people"; "my stay in Ann Arbor was among the happiest periods of my life" (89–90).

It was also the period when Wu came into his own as a scholar. In March 1921, he published his first essay, "Reading from Ancient Chinese Codes and Other Sources of Chinese Law and Legal Ideas," in the *Michigan Law Review*. Aside from being, as he put it, his "maiden work of jurisprudence," the essay also happened to bring about a long friendship with the Supreme Court Justice Oliver Wendell Holmes Jr. Wu, in his typically precocious way, sent the article to Holmes directly, with a note saying that ancient China's legal ideas were similar to Holmes's own. Holmes received the essay but famously replied before reading it, admonishing Wu that

> *one cannot jump at once to great ends. Therefore I hope that you will not shirk the details and drudgery that life offers, but will master them as the first step to bigger things. One must be a soldier before one can be a general. (Zhang 204)*

Holmes, of course, had taken Wu for a much younger student who was punching above his intellectual weight. Once Holmes actually read the essay, however, he immediately sent another note with an apology that read, "I . . . perceive that I am addressing a scholar who already knows so much that he probably smiles at elementary counsels. I trust that you will take my ignorance in good part" (Wu Beyond East, 88–89).

Wu, of course, was thrilled that Holmes, a "grand old man of eighty," had taken an interest in his work. They would continue to correspond for the rest of Holmes's life, exchanging personal and professional advice, discussing their theological differences, and offering critiques and feedback on scholarship in progress. This friendship must have been nearly as much an education for Wu as his law degree, as well as a sign that he was ready to be part of a global dialogue on legal philosophy.

A portrait of Wu. A photograph taken during this session was sent as a gift to Oliver Wendell Holmes Jr. with the dedication, "To my intellectual godfather," 1930. Alumni Association Individual Photos, Bentley Historical Library, University of Michigan.

For several years after his graduation from the U-M Law School in 1921, Wu embarked on a global tour of postgraduate research and study: he went first to the "University of Paris on a fellowship from the Carnegie Endowment of International Peace"; then to Germany and the University of Berlin, where he studied under the "renowned neo-Kantian legal philosopher Rudolph Stammler"; and then finally back to the United States and Harvard Law School for an appointment as a research fellow (Zhang 206).

Not until 1924 did Wu return to China. He had left behind a young wife and family—in the old tradition, they had married young, when Wu was 17, and the marriage had been arranged by Wu's father when Wu was only 6 years old. Now he "was overwhelmed by the joyful reunions":

> *I had a feeling of genuine romance when my two boys, whom I had left as babies, looked suspiciously at me for a long time, as if a stranger had intruded into their home. It was not until my wife told them to greet their "appa" that they jumped into my arms. (Wu Beyond East, 107)*

He settled into a job at his old alma mater, the Comparative Law School of China, teaching law classes that ranged from legal philosophy to Roman law (Zhang 207).

Three years after his return to Shanghai, Wu's public profile rose dramatically. First, the Comparative Law School "appointed him first principal," with the dean citing him as "a brilliant but somewhat unpredictable genius" (Zhang 209). In this position, Wu did much to expand both the school's curricula and the library, joined the advisory board for the new *China Law Review*, and founded the *TienHsien Monthly*, a magazine "aimed at promoting cultural understanding" (210). But the biggest jump in visibility was Wu's 1927 appointment as the chief justice of the Provisional Court of Shanghai. The 1926 Agreement replaced the old mixed court with the new provisional court and signaled a push for greater legal sovereignty.

Wu was positively ecstatic about the opportunities that this new position would afford. He wrote, "I shall have much opportunity of doing creative work in the law! I shall try to Holmesianize the law of China!" (Wu 113). Here at last was a chance to put his learning into practice. The foreign community of Shanghai, however, was not pleased by this pushback against extraterritoriality. They "doubted whether Chinese judges would be able to rule wisely and impartially, whether China had an established legal system with effective laws, and whether the Chinese court system would be corrupt" (Zhang 213).

Wu accepted these challenges and quickly won the public over. The year "1927 was the happiest year of my public life," he wrote. "I felt I was moulding the law of China to my judicial opinions." Two years later, Wu was made president of the provisional court. He had earned the respect of the locals, who wouldn't take money from his wife when

Wu (seated, second from left) with Roscoe Pound (seated, second from right), the dean of Harvard's Law School, and four other dignitaries and officers of the Comparative Law School. At the Comparative Law School, Shanghai, ca. 1935. Courtesy of Historical and Special Collections, Harvard Law School.

she went shopping, and from the press. After one trial, "an American paper reported the judicial proceedings under the headline of 'Solomon sits in judgment'" (Wu Beyond East, 114). In other words, Wu's

> *decisions demonstrated not only his profound and comprehensive understanding of international law, traditional Chinese laws and principles, as well as recently enacted Chinese laws and—more importantly—the relationship among them, but also his ability to apply laws into practice, taking appropriate circumstances into account.* (Zhang 213)

He had put to rest Shanghai foreigners' fears about the competency of the Chinese legal system.

But by 1930, Wu, intellectually and spiritually restless, had left the court to begin a private law practice in Shanghai. "In one month," he wrote, he earned more "than all the salaries I had got as a judge and as a professor put together" (Wu Beyond East, 133). This began a several-year slide into, as he described it, external prosperity and inner depravity:

> *Gradually my clients began to invite me to attend their parties in the "flowery houses," and I offered parties in the same places in return. Before I realized it I had become a regular play-boy. For two and a half years I was out practically every night. Even to think of those days smells hell. (133–134)*

These dark days were intensified by a feeling of estrangement from his wife: "Having nothing in common between us, I felt an utter loneliness at home." Wu felt that the chaos of his personal life reflected "the chaotic conditions of the country" (135).

In 1933, Wu was given the opportunity of a lifetime to help ease these chaotic conditions. He dropped his law practice in Shanghai and entered instead the Republic of China's Legislative Yuan: "Widely known for his legal acumen, panoramic knowledge of foreign legal systems, and unwillingness to entertain bribes, Wu was named Vice-Chair of the . . . Constitutional Drafting Committee and charged . . . with drafting a new Constitution for China" (Alford and Shen 50). For a third time, Wu buried himself in his work. He reviewed the constitutions of other nations, including "the United States, Germany, France, Japan"; he studied the "philosophies of Montesquieu, Rousseau, Lolme, and James Wilson" (Zhang 215–216). The final draft prioritized the three principles of Nationalism, democracy, and livelihood, reflecting "a balance of individualism and collectivism, a hope of synthesizing idealism and materialism" (216). Wu's draft of the constitution, however, was not implemented for many years, and when it was finally adopted, it only survived momentarily before the Chinese Communist Party wrested control of the country from the Nationalists.

In the meantime, Wu and his family focused on surviving the Second World War. They stayed for a time in occupied Shanghai, having lived through the initial invasion and bombardment. But scrutiny against Wu grew as he was invited by the occupying forces to take a seat on a "representative council" (Wu 278). He refused the position, citing his loyalty to China, and while his refusal had no immediate consequences, Wu knew that the time had come to leave the city. Wu and his family registered themselves as laborers under fake names, dressed up "in the most shabby clothes you can imagine," and drove out of the city in a borrowed truck. Wu left behind a poem for the Japanese officer assigned to watch him, sealed in an envelope on his desk for the officer to find. In his autobiography, the only lines Wu could recall were "Excuse me for going away without saying Goodbye! / Loyalty requires the skipping of minor courtesies" (280).

Wu spent the next several years living in poverty in China's interior, sustaining his family only on a wage he earned for a Chinese translation of the Bible, commissioned directly by Generalissimo Chiang Kai-shek. But despite the shabby living conditions, Wu was happy:

> *My dear friend Lin Yutang, who visited us when he was in Kuelin, said that it was more like a pigsty than a house; yet some of my happiest days were spent there, and I cannot look back on those days without a wistful yearning. (Wu Beyond East, 292-293)*

Wu left China at the end of the civil war. Although his later career drew somewhat on his legal expertise (e.g., serving as a judge on the Permanent Court of Arbitrations in the Hague), Wu spent the second half of his life as enchanted by Catholicism and literature as he had been by law during the first half of his life. He struck up a friendship with Thomas Merton, an American Catholic writer, monk, and mystic; he translated a volume of Tang dynasty poetry into English, as well as the *Daodejing*; he wrote books on Zen and Chinese philosophy, which were published in Taiwan and later in the West.

Taken as a whole, Wu's life and career ranged across many disciplines and interests, with far-reaching consequences for China's legal tradition, the Republic's independence from foreign powers, and Western understanding of Chinese culture. His life's work transcended the divisions between East and West, although Wu himself was as ambitious and turbulent and brilliant as China itself in the 20th century.

Works Cited

Alford, William P., and Yuanyuan Shen. "'Law Is My Idol': John C. H. Wu and the Role of Legality and Spirituality in the Effort to Modernise China." *Essays in Honor of Wang Tieya*. Ed. Ronald Macdonald. Norwell, MA: M. Nijhoff Publishers, 1994. Print.

Chun, Allen. "From Text to Context: How Anthropology Makes Its Subject." *Cultural Anthropology* 15.4 (2000): 570–595. Print.

Gao, Yugong. "Cranes and People in China: Culture, Science, and Conservation." Master's thesis, U of Texas at Austin, 2001. Print.

Grimm, Robert J., and Cheng Tso-Hsin. "Special Report: Ornithology in the People's Republic of China (PRC)." *Condor* 81.1 (1979): 104–109. Print.

Hsu, J. P. "The Scientific Research and Teaching of Dayou Wu." *JingShin Theoretical Physics Symposium in Honor of Professor Dayou Wu*. Singapore: World Scientific Publishing, 1998. Print.

Hsu, Weishu. "In Memoriam: Tso-Hsin Cheng, 1906–1998." *Auk* 116.2 (1999): 539–541. Print.

Rank, Michael. "Birdman of Beijing." *Guardian*, 18 July 1998. Print.

Seitz, Frederick. "China and Natural Science: A Conundrum in Remembrance of Professor Ta You Wu (1907–2000)." *Proceedings of the American Philosophical Society* 146.1 (2002): 1–17. Print.

Wu, Dayou. "Reminiscences of My Ann Arbor Days." *JingShin Theoretical Physics Symposium in Honor of Professor Dayou Wu*. Singapore: World Scientific Publishing, 1998. Print.

Wu, Jingxiong. *Beyond East and West*. New York: Sheed and Ward, 1969. Print.

"Wu Ta-you: Biography." *Ramon Magsaysay Award Foundation*. Web. 15 June 2017. <http://www.rmaward.asia/awardees/wu-ta-you/>.

Yang, Chen Ning. "Professor T. Y. Wu and Physics." *Chinese Journal of Physics* 35 (1997): 737–741. Print.

Zhang, Xiaomeng. "John C. H. Wu and His Comparative Law Pursuit." *International Journal of Legal Information* 41.2 (2013): 196–221. Print.

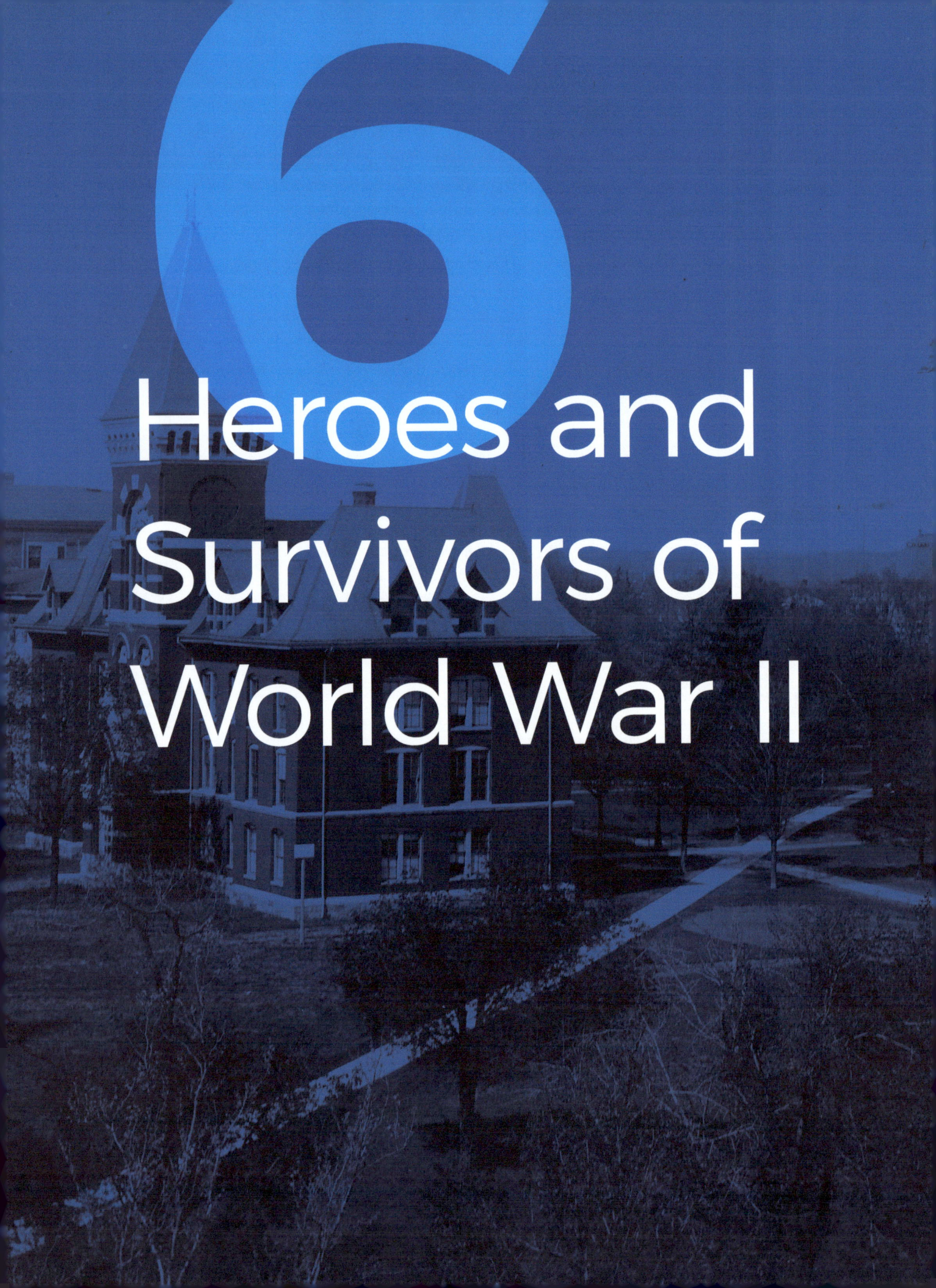

6

Heroes and Survivors of World War II

In the summer of 1937, an armed conflict between Chinese and Japanese forces at the Marco Polo Bridge near Beijing ignited the Second Sino-Japanese War. For the next four years, the Japanese invasion raged down China's eastern seaboard. One by one the biggest cities fell—Beijing, Nanjing, Shanghai—even though China's Communist and Nationalist forces had achieved a nominal and temporary truce, uniting to push back against the Japanese army.

During the early years of the war, the United States remained militarily neutral, although the Roosevelt administration opposed Japanese imperialism and, as the invasion advanced unchecked, American public opinion swung in China's favor. In 1941, the Japanese bombed Pearl Harbor. The United States, no longer able to stay neutral, declared war on Japan, thus cementing an alliance with the Republic of China and enmeshing the Sino-Japanese War once and for all in the larger fabric of World War II.

This book has already described some of the heroes and survivors of World War II: Ding Maoying's efforts as a relief worker and hospital director, Wu Yifang's leadership as the president of Ginling College, and John C. H. Wu's work on China's constitution and escape from Shanghai, to name a few—all deserve to be remembered for providing support during years marked by tragedy.

This chapter tells the story of three graduates from the University of Michigan (U-M) who made contributions during the war years: He Yizhen, one of the first women in China to receive a PhD in physics; Robert Brown, a doctor and missionary who dedicated himself to serving the wounded of WWII; and Tom Harmon, a star Michigan football player who became an air force pilot fighting in China with the Flying Tigers.

He Yizhen: "Studying to Save the Country"

He Yizhen was born into a family tradition of radical scholarship. Her grandmother, Xie Changda, "was known in Suzhou for her feminist activism"—she raised funds to establish a school for women and "founded the Unbinding Foot Society in 1902" (Ma 85). He Yizhen's father, He Cheng, participated in the Xinhai Revolution of 1911 that overthrew the Qing dynasty. In an interview with He Yizhen's daughter, Ge Yunpei, for the documentary *25 Words*, Ge summed up her grandfather's values: "Although my grandfather went to a military college, he never thought of rescuing China by force," she said. "Instead, he believed in natural science and believed that science and industry could rescue the country."

He Cheng passed on this conviction to his eight children. He Yizhen, as the firstborn, was the first of her siblings to carry on this family legacy. She studied at the school in Suzhou that her grandmother had founded and then attended Jinling College, where Wu Yifang, herself a graduate of the University of Michigan, had just become China's first female college president. He graduated in 1930 at just 20 years old and the following year made the decision to continue her studies abroad. The story goes that He's "father gave her money and said 'you can use this money to get married or you can study abroad,'" and the choice was not a difficult one. She studied first at Mount Holyoke College in the United States and then received a Barbour Fellowship to the University of Michigan's PhD program in physics. When she graduated from U-M in 1937, He Yizhen became one of the first women in China to ever receive an advanced degree in physics.

It was during her years abroad that He Yizhen's studies took on a political significance. In 1931, shortly after she arrived in the United States, the Mukden Incident occurred. A staged attack on a Japanese railway in Manchuria by fake Chinese "dissidents," the Mukden Incident gave Japan an excuse to invade Manchuria. He Yizhen's daughter recalled that when "she heard the news of the Mukden Incident . . . she was deeply shocked by the news, and from that time on her ideal of studying to save the country began to take form" (*25 Words*). This idea spread throughout He's family. Her younger sister, He Zehui, followed in Yizhen's footsteps, traveling to Germany to study ballistics.

He Yizhen returned home to teach. Yanjing University hired her to teach graduate courses in physics, and it was there that she met her husband, Ge Tingsui, a graduate student at Yanjing. They married in 1941 and moved back to the United States so that Ge could study at University of California, Berkeley. With Yizhen in the United States, Zehui in Germany, and the rest of their family in China, communication during the war years was difficult. The only possible communication was via the Red Cross, which had implemented a letter service for citizens of war-torn countries. The only catch

He Yizhen (center) surrounded by her younger siblings. Courtesy of 25words.net.

He Yizhen (seated, far right) with her Barbour cohort, 1935. Barbour Scholarship for Oriental Women Committee Records, Bentley Historical Library, University of Michigan.

was that the letters could only be 25 words long, and they were censored for anything but personal content. One such letter from He Yizhen to her family survives. It reads:

> Granddaughter born March 30th in Berkeley.
> All well. Tingsui awarded University fellowship.
> Financially good. How is everybody at home? (*25 Words*)

Soon, however, all correspondence ceased. He Zehui wrote letter after letter from her school in Germany, writing to her sister about the garden she kept, increasingly anxious for a response. No reply came, not to Zehui or to the rest of the He family. It wasn't until the war ended that they learned the truth: shortly after graduating, Yizhen's husband, Ge Tingsui, had been hired on at the Manhattan Project to study radar technology. And even though no communication had been allowed to leave America's top-secret nuclear program, He Yizhen received all of her family's letters and kept them the rest of her life (*25 Words*).

He Yizhen and her husband stayed in the United States for several years after the end of World War II, with Ge Tingsui transferring to the Massachusetts Institute of Technology to continue his research. Once the civil war in China had ended, however, they moved their family back to their homeland. He Yizhen found her expertise in spectroscopy in high demand in the new People's Republic, and she helped found the Institute of Metal Research at the Chinese Academy of Sciences. She worked to increase the production and quality of steel and iron, her scholarship joining the country's push for rapid modernization and industrialization until she became "China's pioneer in spectroscopy" (*25 Words*).

The Cultural Revolution interrupted He's career. Like many other prominent intellectuals, she was forced into physical labor. As the documentary *25 Words* puts it, "During the ultra-leftist years, the eight He siblings suffered oppression and torment to varying degrees. Yet in their lifetimes, they never gave up their pursuits of science."

Indeed, in the later years of her career, He returned to more theoretical research, studying amorphous physics and metallic glass and founding the Institute of Solid State Physics at

He Yizhen (left) with her younger sister, He Zehui, in 1937, the year of her graduation from the University of Michigan. Courtesy of 25words.net.

the Chinese Academy of Science. In the 1980s and 1990s, she won several awards for her scientific contributions and passed away at the age of 98 in 2008.

Robert Ellsworth Brown: Hero of the Nanjing Massacre

By 1918, Robert Brown had already completed 10 years of higher education, first at Taylor University, then at the University of Illinois, and finally receiving his MD from the University of Michigan. He was 31 years old, and he must have chafed against the safety and inaction of so much schooling. In June 1918, just months after graduating, Brown set sail for China as a medical missionary with the Methodist Church. He threw himself into China during her most fractious period, as the civil war bled into the Japanese invasion and World War II. Robert Brown spent the next 25 years of his life crossing the length and breadth of China, from the malaria-stricken Burma Road, to the Communist Party stronghold in Yan'an, to hospitals in the city of Wuhu in Anhui province. Always he seemed to travel toward danger rather than away, seeking the places he could be of most use.

Brown began his work at the Wuhu General Hospital on the banks of the Yangtze River in southeastern China. Here he provided general medical and surgical expertise before transferring to the Department of Public Health, Pediatrics, and Orthopedics. His first six years were interrupted only in the early 1920s by a brief return to Michigan, where he received another degree in public health. The extra degree paid off: in 1924, Brown was made the superintendent of Wuhu General, a position he kept for more than a decade. During his tenure, Brown did much to serve the hospital and the local community, including hosting famed aviator Charles Lindburgh and persuading him to fly much-needed supplies into China.

But in 1937, Brown's position in Wuhu—just 100 kilometers south of Nanjing—put him squarely in the path of the Japanese invasion. Rather than flee to Hong Kong, retreat farther into China's interior, or return to America, Brown dove headlong into danger. He was "supposedly the first American to stay at his post during the Japanese occupation of Wuhu in the early months of the war" (Homer 7). What's more, "on the days of shelling and street fighting" during the Nanjing Massacre at the end of 1937, Brown

> *had calmly driven through the devastated streets in his battered Ford with a pint-sized American flag flying from its snout, to bring in carload after carload of young women to the hospital compound. Later, he had saved his hospital and the three thousand refugees camped within its protecting walls from the Japanese by refusing, at bayonet point, to give them keys to the compound. (7–8)*

A portrait of Robert Ellsworth Brown. Courtesy of General Commission on Archives and History, United Methodist Church.

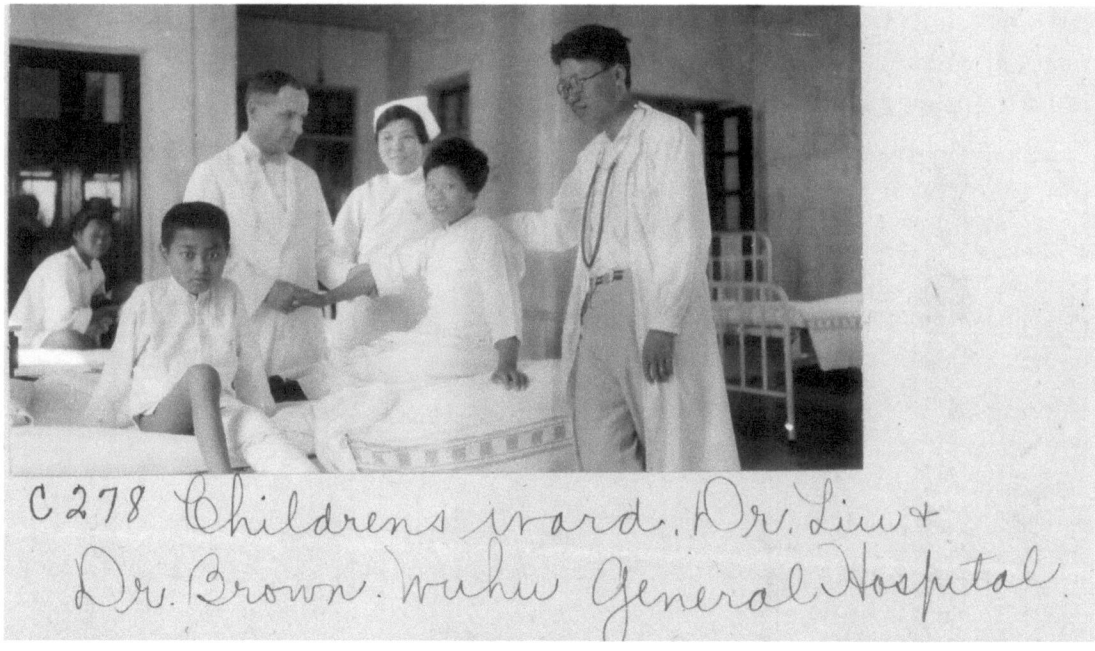

"Children's ward. Dr. Liu and Dr. Brown. Wuhu General Hospital." Courtesy of General Commission on Archives and History, United Methodist Church.

Careless with his own safety, Robert Brown risked his life to shelter and serve thousands of Chinese citizens battered by rape and brutality.

Such efforts did not go unnoticed. He became "something of a hero," and his "reputation in China was public property. . . . He was unofficially titled the best medical administrator in China" (Homer 7–8). Soon Brown was called on to expand his efforts beyond aiding refugees and providing medical administration. Decorated and recognized by Generalissimo Chiang Kai-shek himself, Brown was asked to attend to a new crisis that was developing along the Burma Road.

Built by many thousands of Burmese and Chinese laborers at the start of the war, the Burma Road stretched more than 700 miles from Lashio in Burma to the city of Kunming in China's Yunnan province. The Burma Road was a critical supply line for the Chinese during the Sino-Japanese War, as Burma, then a British colony, funneled much-needed goods into China. While the Japanese army worked to disrupt the supply line through both diplomatic pressure on the British and military advances on Lashio, sickness and disease proved to be nearly an equal threat to the road's success. Malaria, in particular, "made inroads among the Chinese workers," especially in areas where the Burma Road dropped into humid valleys: in one village of 2,000 people, "90% of them were victims of malaria in one season" (Reid 1).

Brown, along with several other health experts, was called in to address the spread of malaria along the Burma Road. Together they analyzed survey data and established two malaria laboratories along the supply route. Brown explained the labs in an interview:

> *These laboratories, while established in very primitive surroundings, have the necessary equipment for the study and control of the malaria problem throughout this district. It is hoped to make these two places demonstration and training centers so that the work can be extended to other points of the Province. (Reid 2)*

In addition to the laboratories, Brown supervised the construction of "a new hospital building at Loiwing" dedicated to the treatment of malaria and the training of Chinese medical staff in the proper care for malaria victims: "At Yuanfu (Kunming) and along the road there are now more than 80 doctors and nurses engaged in health and sanitation work; most of them are well-trained young Chinese." These individuals, Brown said, are the "real pioneers of the new and modern China" (Reid 3).

It was around this time that Robert Brown was joined in China by journalist Joy Homer, who was hired to document the conditions of life in China. Her travel memoirs, published in 1941 as *Dawn Watch in China*, give readers a sense of Brown's character: "He was a broad-shouldered, straight-backed man, with the military carriage and lean blunt features of an army general, rather than a mission doctor" (Homer 5). They traveled together for some thousands of miles, with Brown tasked with coordinating and organizing Christian missions behind the lines and serving as Homer's guide in China. Brown, she soon discovered, was known "throughout the country [as] Skipper" (8).

Homer's account is rich with anecdotes: soon after they began their journey, Brown, arriving at a train station full of sick and injured refugees, turned the station into an "impromptu clinic," bandaging and tending to as many wounded citizens as he could (Homer 26). Later, pausing for several days in the southern city of Guilin, they narrowly survived a Japanese air raid:

> *The next moment the air whined to the scream of falling bombs ... Two hundred yards away in the direction of the hospital, a volcano erupted in brown, heavy coils. Houses just below us sprang outward, thrusting their bellies into the sunny air.... The concussion jerked my fingers, snapped the poised camera. The next bomb would be ours. (55)*

Luckily, the next bomb never came. They recovered and traveled on by train, car, and donkey farther up and farther into China's interior until they arrived in Yan'an, then the primary stronghold of the Chinese Communist Party (CCP), where they met with Mao Zedong. Mao, apparently, gave them a very polite answer as to why the CCP could not allow Christians into its ranks.

When the two of them returned to Brown's old stomping grounds in Wuhu, Homer got a firsthand look at how beloved he was by his former staff and employees:

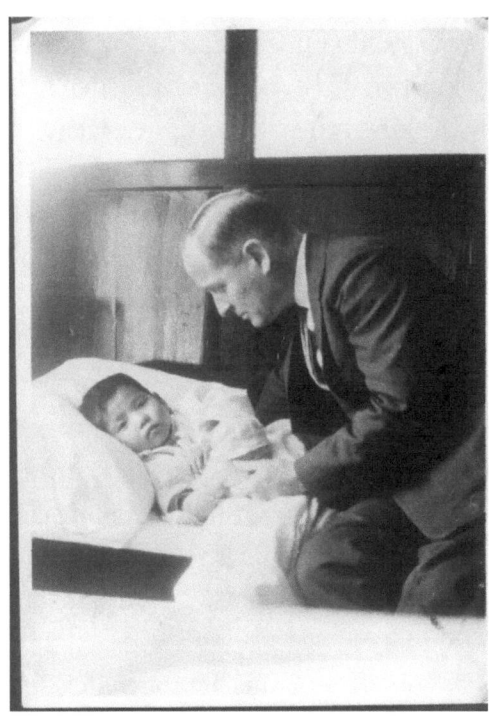

Brown with one of his patients. Courtesy of General Commission on Archives and History, United Methodist Church.

> *Then at last we were being driven through the big walled port of Wuhu, and a half-mile beyond the city to the hill where Robert Brown's gleaming brick hospital towered high and proud above the Yangtze. There must have been close to a hundred people, Americans and Chinese, massed at the compound gate to welcome him. Others crowded the winding road that led up the slope and blacked the lawn upon the hilltop. It was a spectacular homecoming and quite worthy of the Skipper, who was vastly pleased. (Homer 281)*

Joy Homer painted a portrait of Brown in which he was both selfless and irascible, dauntlessly courageous and prone to good-humored jibes. On one occasion, he teased Homer about the fact that she had come down with scarlet fever. On another occasion, Brown himself was the convalescent. Complications from a sinus surgery had laid him low:

> *The doctor told us that another attack would quite definitely be too much for him . . . But I might have known that Skipper would not be so unoriginal as to die. . . . As the hemorrhages gradually stopped, he became a thoroughly unmanageable and indignant patient. When at last he was well enough to get about, we would gladly have thrown him out of his own hospital. (Homer 284)*

Robert Brown left behind a legacy characterized by both a sense of adventure and an unflagging altruism that led him across the length and breadth of China. Brown followed in Judson Collins's footsteps as a missionary from Michigan, and while we recognize now that "missionary" is a complicated calling, Brown seems to have elevated the good and diminished the bad aspects of the position: he was less concerned with evangelism and racial hierarchies and much more concerned with doing good wherever it needed to be done.

When Joy Homer was at last taking her leave of China, Brown

Robert Brown with his family. Courtesy of General Commission on Archives and History, United Methodist Church.

> *was on his way to Rangoon, back to Free China, back to bombings and crumbling roads and flooded rivers. Yet somehow I was not at all worried about Skipper. His own little god of luck perched day and night upon his shoulder. Should a 500 pound bomb fall directly at his feet, it would inevitably turn out to be a dud. (Homer 294)*

HEROES AND SURVIVORS OF WORLD WAR II

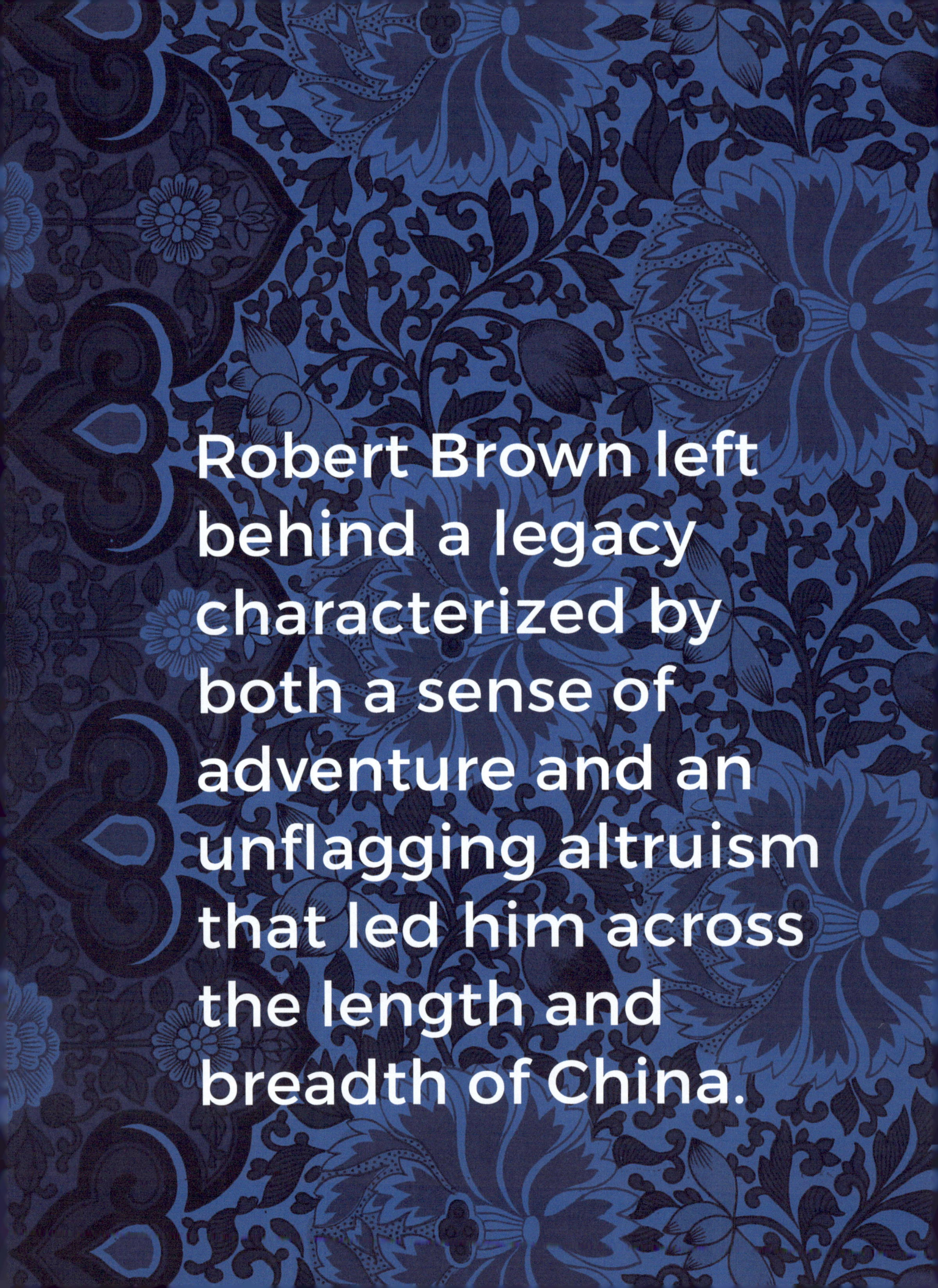

Robert Brown left behind a legacy characterized by both a sense of adventure and an unflagging altruism that led him across the length and breadth of China.

In a tragic irony, Robert Brown survived decades of violent turmoil in China only to die of a heart attack several years after returning home to his family in California.

Harmon of Michigan: Football Star, Fighter Pilot

Tom Harmon was a legend and a national celebrity before he ever set foot in China. A Midwestern boy from a small city in Indiana, Harmon's rise to fame, sacrifice in wartime, courage under fire, and return to the limelight reads like a stereotype of American heroism, the kind of story better suited to Hollywood than the annals of real history. And yet, here it is—Tom Harmon's experience at the University of Michigan and in China, stranger than fiction, blessed by opportunity, luck, and courage in the face of misfortune.

Harmon's star began to rise as soon as he arrived at the University of Michigan. His first memories of the University are of the beauty of its campus:

> *Even today I believe that Ann Arbor in the fall is the most beautiful town in the world . . . The air seemed sort of golden, and the quiet college streets with their big trees were waking up from the drowsy summer as students began to arrive. (Harmon 11)*

Recruited for the football team out of high school, Harmon started his football career on the bench. He had a lot to learn, and while he showed promise as an athlete, Harmon still made crucial, game-losing mistakes. After one especially embarrassing fumble, for Christmas Harmon's family gave him a gift of a football with handles.

His family's teasing surely helped Harmon maintain humility in the success that was soon to follow. By the time he was a sophomore, Harmon had become a star half-back on the University of Michigan team, drawing national press for his performances during high-pressure games against rival schools. "The newspaper boys were laying it on thicker than ever where I was concerned," Harmon wrote. "I tried to tell them that they ought to spread the credit more evenly, for no guy can carry a ball far if the rest of the team isn't in there clearing the way" (Harmon 24). These protests clearly didn't work. He won the Heisman Trophy, was named the Associated Press Athlete of the Year, was inducted into the College Football Hall of Fame, won the Maxwell Award, and appeared on the cover of *Time* magazine—Harmon's photogenic face probably didn't hurt his celebrity status, although teammates and family routinely teased him about his large nose. In his memoir *Pilots Also Pray*, Harmon dismisses this overwhelming catalog of plaudits as "a few other trophies," even as he goes on to describe being invited to meet US president Franklin Delano

Tom Harmon during his football days at U-M, 1940. Alumni Association Records, Bentley Historical Library, University of Michigan.

Roosevelt at the president's birthday ball. In fact, Harmon almost refused the invitation out of fear that missing class would cause him to receive a failing grade, and he only accepted the invitation when a dean stepped in to give him permission.

Harmon's celebrity status only increased after his graduation. To start, he played himself in a Hollywood film called *Harmon of Michigan*. He met actress Elyse Knox, whom he affectionately nicknamed "Butch," and they soon became sweethearts. Harmon was in big demand as a public speaker and traveled across the country giving talks. He sent much of the proceeds back to his parents, eventually buying a house for them in Ann Arbor. In 1940, Harmon was drafted by the Chicago Bears, but he didn't sign a contract in order to pursue a career in radio. He moved in with his parents and went to work as a radio announcer in Detroit.

World War II interrupted Harmon's career ambitions. He enlisted in the air force just months before the bombing of Pearl Harbor and, to his great excitement, was chosen to be a pilot. Boot camp got him back in shape after a year or two off the football field; in no time at all, Harmon had left behind the safety and celebrity of a career in the public eye in order to fly headfirst into combat.

The trouble started on a routine run toward an army base in South America, when his bomber blew a hydraulic line: "No hydraulics fluid meant no brakes." Harmon and his crew managed to patch up the broken line on the fly, and luckily they had enough fluid to let them land safely. The next leg of their journey, however, was not so lucky. As the bomber crew flew across the coast of South America en route to Northern Africa, they ran headlong into a bank of black storm clouds over Devil's Island. Harmon did his best to keep the plane up, avoiding the storm when he could, but just as they entered what seemed to be a break in the clouds, "all hell broke loose. It sounded as though a cannon had gone off. Lt. Wieting yelled: 'The wing! It's tearing off!' I tried desperately to right the ship, but there wasn't much I could do" (Harmon 65). The plane

Harmon registering for the draft, 1941. Athletic Department Records, Bentley Historical Library, University of Michigan.

tipped into a nosedive. Harmon ordered his crew to eject, waiting until his men had gotten clear before ejecting himself.

Harmon awoke to the pouring rain of the South American jungle, the wreck of his bomber still smoldering nearby. His parachute had lodged in a tree on the way down, and now Harmon found himself dangling some 40 feet off the ground. Knowing that too much momentum in the wrong direction could send him plunging to his death, Harmon gingerly swung himself back and forth until he reached the trunk. As he climbed down, the fire in the wreckage reached stores of ammunition, sending live bullets crackling through the underbrush.

Harmon reached solid ground, somehow uninjured, and began to take stock of the situation. Mindful of the exploding ammunition, he searched what was left of the plane for supplies and other survivors. Of the latter, he found only gruesome remains: "I saw an arm that had been torn off at the shoulder," he wrote. "There was a propeller tattooed on it, so I knew it was Sgt. Goodwin's left arm" (Harmon 67). While there was no sign of the rest of his crew, Harmon was able to salvage some equipment: a knife, a mosquito net, a compass, a flare gun, several cans of fresh water, and a chocolate bar that he had left tucked in a pants pocket. Remembering what he could of his navigation maps, Harmon used the compass to pick what he thought was the likeliest direction and started walking.

Harmon was to spend five excruciating days alone in the jungle. At night he slept with the mosquito net draped over his face, though with no way to keep the net propped up, the cloud of insects still managed to get through. He spent sleepless nights under the mosquito net, clutching his knife for fear of wild animals. During the day, Harmon trudged onward, up and down mountains, forcing his way through the underbrush. It was the swamps, however, that gave him the most trouble. More than one of them lay directly in his path and, too wide to circumnavigate, they forced Harmon to wade directly through. The mud sucked at his boots, nearly pulling them off his feet. The water soaked his clothes until he was mud-spattered from head to foot. But worst of all was the lack of food and water. The thought of his candy bar and salvaged water rations kept Harmon going during the arduous first day of walking, but when he at last sat down to rest and opened his supplies, he found that the cans of water had sprung leaks and run empty and that his chocolate bar, carefully saved in his pocket, had been ground into a swampy mash and sprouted maggots.

He carried on like this for five days, each day less certain that the jungle would ever end, each day more weakened by thirst and exhaustion. On the fifth day, Harmon saw something in the foliage that brought him up short: a glass bottle. Reeling and delirious, almost unable to believe his luck, he found a trail in the jungle a short distance away. It led him to a small settlement, part of the larger French colony and the only settlement of its kind for many miles in any direction. Harmon, it seemed, had been saved by luck and providence. He was taken in and given food and a bath. The following day, he was taken upriver by canoe to a larger outpost, from which he was able to transfer to a US military base. In the end, Harmon was the only one of his bomber crew to survive the wreck.

A small thing like crashing a plane into the South American jungle didn't stop Harmon for long. After a brief leave to visit his parents, he returned to active duty. He was to fly a P-38 Lightning, a plane nicknamed the "fork-tailed devil" by pilots in the Luftwaffe. On the side of the plane christened "Butch II" after his girlfriend, Harmon commissioned a painting designed by Walt Disney himself, whom Harmon had befriended in Hollywood: a rendition of the cartoon character Peg-leg Pete, wearing Harmon's football jersey, crushing a swastika in one clawed hand. Harmon was assigned to the 449th Fighter Squadron and shipped to China. Their mission was to support Lieutenant General Claire Chennault, the commander of the famous Flying Tigers. Officially a part of the Chinese Air Force, the Flying Tigers were composed of volunteer pilots from the US Army, Navy, and Marines. And now they had a squadron of new P-38s to provide support for their older P-40 fighters.

Harmon's first reaction to China, just like his first reaction to Ann Arbor, was to marvel at its beauty: "After we got across the mountains, China looked like make-believe land for sure. Everything was green, the countryside smelled fresh" (Harmon 122). The 449th settled in to their new base, somewhat in awe of their Flying Tiger compatriots, many of whom were experienced, war-tested pilots. They exchanged dogfighting strategies, discussed the capabilities and tactics of the Japanese Air Force, and held fierce debates about the relative merits of the P-38s versus the P-40s. The pressure on newer pilots and newer planes to perform well in the Asian theater was palpable to Harmon. "When we first came to China," he wrote, "we knew that a great deal was expected of us. Everybody had heard what a great ship the P-38 was, and we were expected to set the world on fire with it" (132).

The pilots rotated on and off duty, each hoping and fearing that he would see action during his shift. One morning it was Harmon's turn on deck: it was his job to help escort some bombers on a run to disrupt Japanese supply lines along the Yangtze River near Jiujiang—the city where, decades earlier, Kang Cheng and Shi Meiyu had first established their medical practice. This was a low-level mission, a foray of opportunity. As Harmon wrote, the Japanese occupying force in the area had been given "quite a bit of rest," and it was "high time to let them know we were still alive" (Harmon 159). Besides, intelligence had indicated that the Japanese camps in the area only had two planes available for quick deployment—it should have been an easy run.

Harmon in his air force jacket, complete with Disney-designed insignia, 1942. Alumni Association Records, Bentley Historical Library, University of Michigan.

Harmon as a lieutenant with his plane, "Little Butch II," 1941. Athletic Department Records, Bentley Historical Library, University of Michigan.

But as they drew closer to Jiujiang, the pilots saw "that all the streets were cleared and that there was no sign of activity on the ground. The [Japanese] had been warned" (Harmon 162). Enemy fighters screamed up to challenge them, and soon Harmon realized that they were facing not 2 but 6 planes, and then 6 became 12. Badly outnumbered, the 449th Fighter Squadron did their best to fight back and regroup. Harmon described the first moments of the dogfight:

> *The first of the two turned right and dove, while the third one turned left and dove alone . . . I cut loose with the machine gun and the first burst was a lucky shot. It tore the canopy right off . . . and his motor burst into flames. . . . The air now sounded like a million buzzing bees. (163)*

Despite the uneven odds, Harmon and his crew held their own. In the chaos, Harmon took down two, maybe three enemy fighters. Then it was time to disengage:

> *I had climbed steeply in this encounter and was just going to pull over and head for home. Then I heard a sharp ping against the armor plating behind me. Almost*

immediately a second shot hit the armor plate under my seat and I was given a slight jolt. The third shot exploded between my legs. This one blew the gas primer . . . How I missed catching some of those shell splinters I'll never know. (Harmon 163-164)

He avoided the shrapnel, but now the cramped, claustrophobic P-38 cockpit had caught fire. He stamped out the fire as best he could with gloved hands, but the gas line burned too fiercely. In a moment, Harmon's plane was heading "in a ninety degree dive straight for the lake" (Harmon 164). With just seconds to spare, he kicked himself free of the plane and opened his parachute. Except—Harmon had opened his parachute too soon: "My heart went right up into my throat. A man in a parachute is as helpless against a strafing plane as a duck on a string" (165). The best he could do was play dead and hope the Japanese held their fire. Harmon let his head loll. The parachute drifted down into the lake—guiding the parachute to solid ground would have meant giving up the charade. Once in the water, Harmon hid under the parachute cloth until the circling planes flew elsewhere.

Only when the immediate threat had passed did Harmon realize how badly he had been burned: "It hurt, but I wasn't going to let that bother me" (Harmon 165). Somehow, Harmon, wrapped in the remnants of his parachute, swam to shore. Soon guerrilla fighters with the Chinese Communist Party found him. Over the next month, they slowly nursed him back to health and made their way back to Harmon's base camp. The pain of his wounds, so blithely dismissed in the adrenaline of the plane crash, came back with a vengeance: "In those days I went through the most physically painful experience of my life. The burns on my legs and face got infected and festering." Limited medical care on the rural route back to safety meant that Harmon could only treat his burns with tea, using tannin to take some of the sting out. "My face was so badly burned that my eyes and lips were simply swollen shut," he wrote. "Because my mouth was so badly burned, I could hardly eat for 17 days" (166). To make matters worse, Harmon came down with dysentery on the journey home.

Thirty-two days after the fight over Jiujiang and some 40 pounds underweight, Harmon stumbled back into his base camp. A celebration was held to mourn those lost in the fight and to honor Harmon as a survivor. The camp cook baked him a cake with chocolate bars donated by the rest of the squadron—it was, he wrote, the best thing he had ever tasted.

Tom Harmon of Michigan returned home a hero. He was awarded a Purple Heart, married his Hollywood sweetheart, played football in the NFL for several seasons before recognizing that his war injuries had marred his physical fitness, and eventually became a professional sports broadcaster. He died in 1990 at the age of 70, a hero and a survivor of World War II.

Fritz Crisler (right), U-M football coach, with Harmon's parents and sister, reading the news that Harmon had survived being shot down in China, 1943. H. O. Crisler Papers, Bentley Historical Library, University of Michigan.

Tom Harmon with his wife, actress Elyse "Butch" Knox, 1951. Alumni Association Records, Bentley Historical Library, University of Michigan.

Works Cited

25 Words. Directed by Shen Liu. 2011.

Harmon, Tom. *Pilots Also Pray*. New York: Crowell, 1944. Print.

Homer, Joy. *Dawn Watch in China*. Boston: Houghton Mifflin, 1941. Print.

Ma, Yuxin. *Women Journalists and Feminism in China, 1898-1937*. Amherst, NY: Cambria Press, 2010. Print.

Reid, W. W. "Interview with Robert Brown." Robert Brown Collection, Bentley Historical Library, U of Michigan, 1940. Print.

7

Postwar Scientists in the People's Republic of China

In the years following World War II, China's efforts to modernize science and medicine in the new People's Republic were complicated. On one hand, China's headlong rush into the industrial age meant that the country relied, more than ever, on the research done by scientists newly minted in Western universities. The value placed on practical research combined with the verve and patriotism inspired by the promise of a new government meant that mid-20th-century China could be an exciting place for scientists who wanted to see their work change the world. On the other hand, however, institutes of higher learning were subject to the caprice of Chairman Mao and party politics. What began during the Great Leap Forward as preferential treatment for certain disciplines and doctrines became, during the Cultural Revolution, a vilification of many of the country's brightest minds.

Graduates from the University of Michigan (U-M) experienced both ends of this spectrum, from Wang Chengshu and Zhu Guangya, physicists whose work on China's nuclear program brought them security and prestige, to Huang Jiasi and Zeng Chengkui (C. K. Tseng/Zeng), a surgeon and a marine biologist, respectively, who both suffered as their work came to a halt during the Cultural Revolution. But with or without the blessing of the People's Republic, all four scientists accomplished great things for the people of China.

Wang Chengshu and Zhu Guangya: Pioneers of China's Nuclear Age

In August 1946, Mao Zedong met with American journalist Anna Louise Strong in the Chinese Communist Party (CCP) stronghold in Yan'an. The Second World War had just ended in the fires of America's atomic bombs, but peace was not yet on the horizon for China, whose civil war between the CCP and the Nationalists had flared to life again. During his conversation with Strong, Mao was famously dismissive of the atomic power that had just ended WWII: "All reactionaries are paper tigers" (Zhang 195).

Such a dismissal could have been bravado, misdirection, or a genuine belief that military might came from the people rather than from technological advancements. And yet, as early as 1949, "a CCP delegation in Moscow headed by Liu Shaoqi, supposedly requested—but was denied—a tour of Soviet nuclear installations" (Horsburgh 41). With the Communist Party's victory over Chiang Kai-shek's Nationalists, Mao's ambitions had room to grow. Having created a sovereign Communist nation, he set his sights on establishing China as one of the world's superpowers. In a 1956 essay, "Mao connected economic construction with defence construction," ultimately planning to step out from under the USSR's protective nuclear umbrella. China needed an atomic program of its own—the threat of the United States' nuclear arsenal during the Korean War and the Taiwan Straits Crises in the early 1950s had proven just how powerful a symbol and a deterrent nuclear weapons could be. In 1955, Mao formally inaugurated China's nuclear weapons program. A call went out to "expatriate and foreign trained scientists": China was joining the nuclear age (42).

Two students from the University of Michigan answered this call. One, Wang Chengshu, had already been studying physics for a decade and a half before the end of World War II. She received her bachelor's degree in 1934 and then a master's in physics in 1936 from Yen-ch'ing University in Beijing. Wang made her living during the war years as an instructor, working as a lecturer first at her alma mater before, like so many others, moving inland during the Japanese invasion, where she continued teaching at Xiangya Medical College in Changsha (Wang 256). In the autumn of 1939, Wang married Zhang Wenyu, himself a professor of physics, but the newlywed couple only had two years together before life interfered.

In 1941, Wang left her husband and her war-torn country behind to study at the University of Michigan on a Barbour Fellowship. In an interview with the *Ann Arbor News* that December, Wang said that she hoped to be reunited with her husband in three to four years. "Our sacrifice is not so important," Wang said, "if we can return and aid in the rebuilding of China." She described the condition of education in the war years, telling the reporter about multiple universities relocating and sharing buildings, about students "living and studying in caves where they can hide when planes fly overhead." The contrast of her experience—with the convenience of a modern dormitory and the expanse of the University's facilities—with the poor conditions plaguing her husband and their friends must have been difficult. "Of course, we feel terrible," she said, "to think that our friends and relatives at home are suffering through want of food and some of them are even dying. . . . If I keep busy," she continued, "it is easier to forget."

Wang Chengshu (top row, left) with her Barbour cohort, 1942. Barbour Scholarship for Oriental Women Committee Records, Bentley Historical Library, University of Michigan.

"Keep busy" is one way to put it. Wang quickly became one of the top students in her program, studying under famous Dutch theoretical physicist George Uhlenbeck, with whom she would write and publish several papers. She received her PhD in 1945 and stayed on at Michigan as a research fellow for the next 10 years. Wang "conducted research into statistical mechanics and the kinetics of inert gases. She is credited with an adjustment to the Boltzmann equation . . . in polyatomic gases that resulted in it being renamed the WC-U equation" (Wang 526). In total, during her time at the University of Michigan, Wang published more than 10 research papers—and her career was just beginning.

Several years after arriving in America, Wang's hope of reuniting with her husband was realized. Zhang Wenyu had himself come to the United States, appointed first by Princeton and then Purdue University as a visiting research professor. The end of the 1940s saw China, under the banner of the People's Republic, united and whole for the first time in decades, and both Wang and her husband ached to return home. It was years, however, before they could leave the country, due to "American regulations in force during the early years of the Cold War" that forbade the travel of Chinese

Wang (left) in the lab at U-M. Barbour Scholarship for Oriental Women Committee Records, Bentley Historical Library, University of Michigan.

nationals (Lee). Not until 1956, with their young son in tow, were Wang and her husband permitted to return home.

Back in the People's Republic, the role of science in creating an international superpower was finally being reflected in government budgets. At a time when many millions of citizens were sliding toward famine, "funds for science rose from about US $15 million in 1955 to about US $100 million in 1956; the Chinese Academy of Sciences received three times as much money in 1957 as it had received in 1953" (Lewis and Xue 42). Wang found that her new skills and expertise were in high demand. The Chinese Academy of Sciences used some of their new funds to appoint her as researcher at their Institute of Physics in Beijing, a position she held for eight years (at one point even holding a second faculty position at Peking University).

Wang's real contribution to the legacy of New China, however, was about to begin. In 1964, Wang was chosen to work at the Third Research Institute of the Ministry of Nuclear Industry. This move brought her directly into the arms of the nuclear program, where she was put "in charge of the diffusion process to enrich uranium" (Wang 261). Such an important position offered some shelter for Wang during the difficult years of the Cultural Revolution, which would begin in earnest in 1966. In fact,

> *what appears to have protected many scientists in the nuclear program is not their association with the program as such, but the physical isolation that came with it. In the early 1960s, for example . . . Wang Chengshu "[was] successively transferred to engage in the development of the strategic weapons program." . . . From then on, "they left the metropolitan areas for the Gobi desert, the snowy mountains and the grasslands, and, keeping their identities hidden, quietly immersed themselves in hard work." The moment they passed into that program's secret world, they fell under the military's control.* (Lewis and Xue 46)

Wang's work with the nuclear industry carried her into the mid-1970s, when she rejoined the world of academia. Ultimately, Wang balanced her work as an instructor and as a government researcher, serving as a professor for Tsinghua University and as chief engineer in the Ministry of Nuclear Energy's Department of Technology, where she continued her research on uranium isotopes. Ultimately, Wang Chengshu is justly remembered as a key scientist in China's burgeoning nuclear program, "not least through the research theoreticians she trained in uranium isotopes separation studies" (Wang 527).

The second student from the University of Michigan to have a hand in China's nuclear program was Zhu Guangya. While Zhu, like Wang Chengshu, was trained as a scientist and received advanced degrees in physics, he played a primarily administrative role in the development of the atomic bomb.

Zhu seems to have been handpicked for leadership. During the war years, Zhu graduated from and then taught at Southwest China Associated University, the conglomerate of schools that had fled inland from the Japanese invasion. There he met Professor Wu Dayou (see chapter 5), himself an alumnus of the University of Michigan. When WWII ended and Wu was invited back to U-M as a visiting scholar, Wu suggested that Zhu Guangya accompany him, and "that invitation became Zhu's ticket to America and a doctorate in nuclear physics at the University of Michigan" (Lewis and Xue 145). The birth of the People's Republic during Zhu's years as a student at U-M invigorated him just as it did Wang Chengshu, then a research fellow in the same department. In the first year of the People's Republic, Zhu went so far as to coauthor an open letter to all Chinese nationals studying abroad, exhorting them to return home to the motherland.

Zhu followed his own advice, returning to China as soon as he graduated with his PhD in nuclear physics in 1950. Just a year after achieving sovereignty, the People's Republic of China (PRC) was already facing its first international crisis. The invasion of

Zhu Guangya (left) in 1947 at the University of Michigan with, from left, Zhang Wenyu, C. N. Yang, and T. D. Lee. Yang and Lee, both students of Wu Dayou, won the Nobel Prize in 1957. Courtesy of the People's Publishing House, China.

South Korea by North Korea grew quickly from a territorial dispute into a battleground for political ideologies, with Russia and the People's Republic providing support to their Communist North Korean allies and the United States and the UN supporting South Korea. China and the United States, so recently allied during World War II, found themselves on opposite sides of the battlefield. But it was precisely Zhu Guangya's experience in the United States that brought him into this conflict. He was called away from his teaching position to serve as a translator on behalf of the Chinese People's Volunteers during armistice talks (Ni).

Zhu Guangya with his wife, Xu Huijun, in America, 1950. Photo courtesy of the People's Publishing House, China.

Zhu Guangya with his wife, Xu Huijun, in front of the North-Eastern People's University. Courtesy of the People's Publishing House, China.

By the mid-1950s, Mao and the People's Republic had jump-started their nuclear weapons program. Mao's "paper tiger" doctrine had evolved:

> *We are stronger than before and will be still stronger in the future. We will have not only more planes and artillery but atomic bombs as well. If we are not to be bullied in this present-day world, we cannot do without the bomb. (Lewis and Xue 142)*

In 1955, Zhou Enlai himself, China's premier, ordered "the Ministry of Education to form a Nuclear Education Leading Group," and Zhu Guangya was one of several professors who was called on to organize a physics curriculum at Beijing University (106). After this job, it wasn't long before Zhu found a home working for the Ninth Bureau, the top-secret nuclear weapons program. When he first joined in 1959, Zhu assisted in the "management of scientific research" (145).

The Ninth Bureau, meanwhile, was scouting locations for a secret research facility: "Few outsiders ever knew of the academy, and those who did, if they spoke of it at all, referred to it only by its code name, the Ninth Academy" (Lewis and Xue 141). After several years of difficult construction during a time of famine, the Ninth Academy was completed in the remote western reaches of Qinghai province "'on a plateau where the air is thin and people breath[e] with difficulty [and] feel dizzy and asthmatic after they have taken a few steps'" (143). Zhu was one of only four leaders and scientists to helm the administration of this secret facility:

> *As chief of scientific research at the academy, Zhu sought to combine theoretical and applied studies and paid special attention to training in technical quality control. He is remembered for enforcing high scientific standards and for fostering an academy-wide working style that endured into the 1980s. On a state occasion held to pay homage to his achievements in the program, Premier Zhou Enlai singled out Zhu "for his careful and meticulous spirit of work." (145)*

Zhu (right) with Qian Xuesen (left) and Deng Jiaxian (center), two other key contributors to China's nuclear program, 1966. Courtesy of the People's Publishing House, China.

This attention to detail grew ever more significant as China's relationship with Russia deteriorated in the years after Stalin's death in 1953. As advice from Soviet scientists working at the Ninth Academy began to dry up, Chinese researchers had to do more with less. On one occasion, Russian advisers departing the academy left behind some shredded documents, which the Chinese then painstakingly reassembled. Zhu Guangya was called on to explain "the meaning of this 'number-one secret document' to his associates in the academy and [point] out its important clues for their research strategy" (Lewis and Xue 161).

In 1964, after years of labor, difficult timetables, food shortages, and political labyrinths, Zhu Guangya and his colleagues gathered 70 kilometers away from the test site to witness the detonation of China's first atomic weapon. Watching the shockwave unfurl, Zhu and the rest "were overcome with the emotions released after long years of trial. They wept" (Lewis and Xue 188). News of the successful test went out immediately to Zhou Enlai, then on to Chairman Mao, then to the people of Beijing, and finally to the rest of the world.

In the following decades, Zhu Guangya was elected several times to the Central Committee of the Communist Party, served as an academician for the Chinese Academy

Zhu Guangya shakes hands with Chairman Mao Zedong, 1974. Courtesy of the People's Publishing House, China.

Zhu Guangya marking nuclear test research papers. Courtesy of the People's Publishing House, China.

of Sciences, was president of the Chinese Academy of Engineering, and served as the director of the State Administration for Science, Technology and Industry for National Defense.

Huang Jiasi: At the Helm of Surgery in New China

Huang Jiasi (Huang Chia-ssu), a cardiothoracic surgeon in charge of directing large swathes of China's medical education, wrote two essays addressing the international medical community. He wrote them more than 20 years apart: the first just a decade into the life of the PRC, the second some years after the death of Mao Zedong. Both essays aim to take the pulse of medical education in China, and both begin by connecting the work of contemporary surgeons to China's millennia-old tradition of surgery. "In China there has long been coexistence of two schools of medicine, traditional Chinese medicine and modern medicine," he wrote in 1982. In 1959, Huang wrote that "the history of surgery in China dates back as far as the Chou dynasty (1134–770 B.C.), when surgical diseases were described and their treatment became a specialty." As a

Western-educated surgeon working in China, Huang became a part of this lineage, the synthesis of Eastern and Western medicine into a global discipline. It speaks well of Huang's values and convictions that even after the Cultural Revolution's demonization of "the Four Olds," he was willing to connect his own work with the venerable traditions of ancient China.

The story of Huang Jiasi's place in this tradition begins with the ambition and impudence of his older brother. The fourth of eight sons, Huang was raised by his mother and older siblings—his father had died when he was only five years old. While Huang had shown "talent in mathematics and physics in early primary school," by the time he reached high school in 1924, he still hadn't settled on a career path (Wan and Yim 1147). During spring break, he visited one of his older brothers in Beijing, who quizzed Huang on his future. As they strolled past the Peking Union Medical College (PUMC), then a "beautiful . . . Chinese palace style campus in downtown Beijing," Huang's brother asked him if he might like to study there someday: "'Sure,' Huang answered without thinking. Six months later, his brother applied to PUMC on Huang's behalf. 'Your English is good . . . Why not just try so that two years later you can be better prepared for the real examination?'" (1-2). Huang followed his brother's lead, was accepted to PUMC, and took the first steps of a career that would place him at the head of surgery in China.

An oil painting of Huang Jiasi gifted to the Peking Union Medical College in 1985. Courtesy of Chinese University Press Hong Kong.

Huang's education took him from Beijing at the PUMC to the National Shanghai Medical College, where he lectured until 1939. The Japanese invasion displaced Huang and the rest of his university—they retreated first to Kunming and then to Chongqing in southern China. In 1941, he escaped the war entirely. With a scholarship from Tsinghua University funded by the Boxer indemnity, Huang was chosen to study abroad. He arrived in Ann Arbor in mid-October, just in time for Michigan's full flush of autumn, and began the final stage of his education.

At the University of Michigan, Huang studied with John Alexander, who had established "the first surgical residency program in thoracic surgery in the United States." Under Alexander's influence, Huang focused his studies on pulmonary tuberculosis and was "extremely active not only in the operating rooms but also in the laboratory" (Wan and Yim 1148). When Huang received his master's in 1943, he turned down a lucrative position at a military hospital to return home to China. In a twist of irony, Huang's trip back was delayed when he himself contracted pulmonary tuberculosis.

Like Wang Chengshu and Zhu Guangya, Huang's return to China from the United States was accompanied by a swift rise in prestige. In the latter half of the 1940s alone, Huang became a professor at Shanghai Medical College, "the surgeon-in-chief of two hospitals," and the president of the Chinese Surgical Association. When the Korean War broke out in 1950, Huang led a contingent of medical practitioners from Shanghai into service at an army hospital in northeastern China. Huang and his peers did incredible work, performing nearly 1,000 procedures in six months. And yet, the political connotations of this service threatened to rupture Huang's synthesis of East and West. He had been chosen to be one of the founding members of the American Board of Thoracic Surgery, but "'this honor was withdrawn by the Board when it was thought that he supported China during the Korean War,'" and it would be some 28 years before the position was restored to him by the dean of the University of Michigan Medical School (Wan and Yim 1149). In the meantime, Huang reported on his experience during the war at the 1951 National Congress; at the official dinner, Huang was seated next to Chairman Mao Zedong himself.

With his increased authority and visibility, Huang threw himself into the task of developing and reorganizing China's medical practices. In the decade after the Korean War, Huang, already the vice dean of the Shanghai Medical College and president of Zhongshan Hospital, added a third major administrative duty as the "founding president of the Shanghai Chest Hospital, a newly established specialty center for thoracic surgery." The Shanghai Chest Hospital quickly became one of the largest operations of its kind in China and included "the first Chinese made heart-lung machine." Somehow, in the midst of these major leadership positions, Huang Jiasi found time to edit a surgical textbook, the first of its kind in the Chinese language. It was distributed nationwide in 1958 with enough success to warrant additional, reedited runs in 1960 and 1964 (Wan and Yim 1150).

The year 1958 was a landmark year for Huang for another reason: he "was appointed president of the Chinese Academy of Medical Science," a platform that would allow him to create an enduring legacy. His primary task as

Huang Jiasi at a dinner with Chairman Mao Zedong, 1951. Courtesy of Chinese University Press Hong Kong.

head of the organization was to help "build a top-notch medical university similar to that of PUMC" (Wan and Yim 1150). This school, China Medical University, the only eight-year training and education program in the country, opened a year later with Huang as its first president. He held the position for the next 25 years, even through the turmoil of the Cultural Revolution.

Huang's 1981 overview of medical education in China for the *American Journal of Surgery* described the roller coaster of progress in the first decades of the People's Republic. He outlined several successful postrevolution reforms, including the combination and reallocation of medical universities in the hope that their resources might be "more reasonably distributed geographically and their faculties strengthened"; the standardization and "unification of medical educational programs," a process that put in place a national examination for high school graduates applying to medical school; and "the integration of traditional Chinese medicine with Western medicine," such that medical schools worked courses on traditional medicine into their curricula (Huang, "Medical Education" 661). One result of these reforms, Huang wrote, was a massive increase in educated medical practitioners: "The total enrollment of students in secondary medical schools in 1949 was only 15,387, but had increased to 15 times that number—244,695—by 1980" (662).

This progress came to a halt during the years of the Cultural Revolution. Part anti-intellectual campaign, part youthful rebellion gone haywire, part retribution against top-level members of the CCP who had dared to criticize the Great Leap Forward and the famine that followed, Mao Zedong's Cultural Revolution was barely controlled chaos. "Education was completely paralyzed for four years," Huang wrote. It was not uncommon in those years for students-turned-Red Guards to harangue and torment their teachers, sometimes to the point of suicide: "No new student was admitted to any college and all the students in schools participated in political movement day and night" (Huang, "Medical Education" 663).

The eight-year program at China Medical University, once a hallmark of its rigorous education, now came under fire "as the epitome of the overemphasis on professionalism, specialization, and detachment from the real medical problems of a rapidly changing China" (Suttmeier 184). Angry students even composed a song demeaning the school:

These eight years in the old China Medical College—
  The havoc they wrought!
In three years no medicine did we glean;
  In five years no patients were seen;
A full eight years, and no contact with workers and peasants brought! (184)

Even after the worst had passed, "the ideology of the more you learn, the more reactionary you are" lingered on into the 1970s, hampering education and turning out graduates who were "given responsibility they could hardly bear" (Huang, "Medical Education" 663).

Huang, even as his institution came under fire and his life's work was being devalued, never gave up. At the end of the 1970s, he revised and redistributed his seminal *Textbook of Surgery*. He raised funds from the China Medical Board of the Rockefeller Foundation that, by the 1980s, "exceeded $1 million." He also

> reestablished the regular scientific exchanges and collaborations with the Johns Hopkins University and the National Institute of Health in the United States. As a result . . . this university has been repeatedly ranked as one of the top two medical schools in China in the past two decades. (Wan and Yim 1150)

Huang (third from right) in Beijing, 1981. Courtesy of Chinese University Press Hong Kong.

Until the end of his life, Huang Jiasi remained a mentor and a leader whose dedication to serving the people of China never wavered, even in the face of tremendous political turmoil.

Zeng Chengkui: Father of Marine Botany

The arc of Zeng Chengkui's career seems in many ways emblematic of the state of science in mid-20th-century China. Driven from a young age by both intellectual curiosity and political activism, Zeng's enthusiasm for science as a practical discipline aligned him neatly with the goals of the People's Republic. As with many others in this book, Zeng used his education at the University of Michigan as a means to kick-start an entire field back home in China, performing pioneering work in phycology and marine botany. And yet, that same Western education was used as an excuse to torment Zeng during the years of the Cultural Revolution. But like Huang Jiasi working in the medical sector, Zeng refused to tear at the seams, holding on resolutely to his synthesis of East and West.

Born just two years before the 1911 revolution that overthrew the Qing dynasty, Zeng grew up in a political milieu that encouraged political activism and empathy for the working poor. While he was sheltered by his family's wealth from the worst of the chaos during the years of warlordism, Zeng couldn't help but witness

> the abject poverty of peasants in Xiamen (Amoy), an island city on the East China coast. He took his countrymen's plight to heart, changing his name to "Ze-Nong"—which means "to benefit the peasants"—when he was in high school. (Neushel and Wang 62–63)

During his college years, Zeng was expelled from Fujian Christian University for participating in a strike against the administration, which had refused to register with the new Nationalist government.

Leaving Fujian behind and enrolling at Xiamen University, Zeng discovered a discipline that channeled his political leanings into scientific curiosity. Several botany and phycology courses "inspired Zeng's interest in 'agriculture in the sea.'" Here was a topic that might directly alleviate the suffering of the peasants and fishermen working on the rest of the island. He wasted no time in becoming an assistant for the Department of Biology, which sent him around the island gathering algae samples. Zeng saw firsthand how coastal villagers were already harvesting and cultivating algae and seaweed for food and fertilizer. A particular species, *chicai*, caught his attention: "By scraping the rocks with knives and other tools several times a year they eliminated algal competitors and thereby encouraged the natural growth of *chicai*" (Neushel and Wang 63). Already Zeng's attention was almost as much anthropological as botanical—this early research prefigured his later contributions, where the utility of phycology was never far from Zeng's mind.

Portrait of Zeng, 1946. Courtesy of Scripps Institution of Oceanography Photographs, University of California–San Diego.

He took this interest into graduate school at Lingnan University, where, on a fellowship from the Rockefeller Foundation (founder of Peking Union

Medical College, in which Huang Jiasi was trained), he published his first paper on *chicai*. During these years of study, Zeng had to build his own foundation of knowledge: "Unlike scientists interested in terrestrial agriculture, Zeng had no body of published information to work from." He embarked on a long series of trips up and down China's coast, "often traveling alone under difficult conditions," with the goal of establishing a taxonomy of China's marine algae: "Before I could do anything in my choice of seaweed cultivation, I should be familiar with their names," Zeng said (Neushel and Wang 64).

Zeng earned his master's of science degree in 1934 and worked for several years as a lecturer before deciding continue his studies in the United States. At the University of Michigan, studying under William R. Taylor, Zeng drove himself to work at breakneck speed, "often spending nineteen-hour days in the laboratory." During his years of studying abroad, crises at home drew his attention back to China. His family, still living on the eastern seaboard, was endangered by the Japanese occupation—Zeng asked "friends to smuggle them to a safer part of the country." Meanwhile, several marine biological stations, impressed by Zeng's work and "eager for [him] to return home, offered him directorships" (Neushel and Wang 66). But with the bombing of Pearl Harbor and the United States' entry into the war, returning home would have been a difficult, delayed process. Zeng decided to stay in the United States, winning a postdoctoral fellowship from U-M to continue his studies on the West Coast. He wouldn't return home until the war had ended.

Zeng's interest in applied research flourished in his postdoctorate years. The war with Japan meant that imports of agar, a derivative of red algae, had run dry, and Zeng was approached by the Department of Agriculture and the US Fish and Wildlife Service to help find alternative sources. Zeng embraced this opportunity, even though it meant altering the focus of his postdoctorate research. The move brought some friction between Zeng and his mentor at the University of Michigan, William Taylor, who "did not share his former pupil's enthusiasm for applied research" (Neushel and Wang 67). In a letter that autumn, Zeng defended the shift in focus:

> *Like all other sciences, [phycology's] value lies in its cultural [worth] as well as its relationship with the human race in a way. Again like all other sciences, it should be brought closer to the general populace, whenever possible, especially during the war time. (68)*

Zeng dove, literally, into his research, performing underwater surveys of marine algae. Professional divers taught him to use their equipment, and soon Zeng was making monthly dives 30 feet deep in the ocean, despite the near disaster of his first dive, during which "a malfunctioning air valve leaked water into his suit as he stood on the ocean floor" (Neushel and Wang 68–69). The research was a success—the United

The arc of Zeng Chengkui's (C. K. Tseng) career seems in many ways emblematic of the state of science in mid-20th-century China.

Zeng as a postdoc at Scripps Institution of Oceanography. Courtesy of Scripps Institution of Oceanography Photographs, University of California–San Diego.

States, he discovered, had a wealth of red algae to rival Japan's. Moreover, "Zeng's in-the-ocean approach to marine phycology helped transform it from a descriptive to an experimental science. . . . By the end of the war, Zeng was a leading authority not only on the distribution but also on the processing of marine algae" (69).

After the end of the Japanese occupation and World War II, Zeng returned home to China, accepting a position "as professor and chair of the Department of Botany at the National University of Shandong," which had "promised to allocate $15,000 for

Zeng in a diving suit at Laguna Beach, California. Courtesy of Scripps Institution of Oceanography Photographs, University of California–San Diego.

Zeng with Professor Marston Sargent collecting Gellidium seaweed, ca. 1946. Courtesy of Scripps Institution of Oceanography Photographs, University of California–San Diego.

the purchase of research equipment" (Neushel and Wang 71). Still, Zeng was not prepared for the devastation the war had wrought in his home country. "I never realized we had lost so heavily," Zeng wrote. As the new chair, it was up to him to bring his department back to life. "For many weeks . . . I plunged, body and soul, into organizing the department," he wrote (72). This meant everything from hiring new faculty to ordering basic equipment to making chairs by hand. When he had the department back in a semblance of working order, he only had to wait for an end to the civil war. In a 1947 letter, Zeng wrote, "Spring is coming, and the flowers of *Prunus yezoensis* will come out in another week or two. Everything will be lovely, and we hope the same will be true with the Chinese political and economic situation!" (73).

As the civil war raged, Zeng didn't find himself strongly aligned with either the Nationalists or the Communists. The former he found to be "corrupt" and inefficient; the latter, a breeding ground for "extremists" (Neushel and Wang 73). Unlike many of his peers, however, Zeng did not flee to Taiwan when it became clear that the Nationalist cause was doomed. He and his department decided to give the new Communist government the benefit of the doubt.

This "wait and see" approach payed immediate dividends. The prompt creation of the Chinese Academy of Sciences (CAS) in 1949 "impressed Zeng" (Neushel and Wang 74). He had been invited to attend the conference during which the academy was conceptualized, and soon his department at the University of Shandong was folded into the CAS umbrella as the Marine Biological Laboratory of the Chinese Academy of Sciences. The early 1950s saw an explosion of research in their new laboratory. Keeping in mind Premier Zhou Enlai's rejoinder to "bring about close coordination between academic research and practical needs," Zeng guided the Marine Biological Laboratory in researching several species of algae growing along China's coastline. In particular, *Laminaria japonica* (kelp, or *haidai*) drew his attention for its utility as both a fertilizer and a food source. Over the next six years, Zeng and his research group solved the biological and engineering problems standing in the way of ocean farming. By the mid-1950s, Zeng was ready to share large-scale cultivation of *Laminaria* with the rest of China.

The completion of his research on *Laminaria* coincided with the People's Republic's Great Leap Forward program. By 1958, the Ministry of Fisheries was organizing training regimens for local fishermen, teaching them Zeng's techniques for *Laminaria* production. They proved to be wildly successful. Zeng and his team worked closely with local farming groups to "modify cultivation techniques to match local conditions," with the end result being that

> *the* Laminaria *farms [were] the rare case where the much—and appropriately—criticized Great Leap Forward policies actually worked. In an amazingly short period, an enormous new industry was created by applying scientific knowledge accumulated by Zeng's research group at the Institute of Oceanology. Annual production of* Laminaria *increased 155 times, from 40.3 dry tons in 1949 to 6,253.23 dry tons in 1958. (Neushel and Wang 79)*

These were life-saving numbers in years otherwise marked by famine. But by the late 1960s and the advent of the Cultural Revolution, the contributions made by Zeng and his team were forgotten. Mao incited a revolutionary fervor in his young Red Guards, exhorting them to "expose the reactionary bourgeois stand of those so-called 'academic authorities' who opposed the party and socialism" (Neushel and Wang 82). The chaos that followed hit the Chinese Academy of Sciences hard. "Among 170 senior CAS scientists in the Beijing area, 131 were attacked," and Zeng's Institute of Oceanology was no exception (83). Zeng himself came under particular scrutiny for having studied in America:

> *Red Guards took over the institute and imprisoned Zeng, a "reactionary academic authority," in his laboratory. He was beaten, starved, placed in solitary confinement, and forced to write confessions about alleged crimes committed by himself and others. Fei recalled that when his mentor was finally released from the* niupeng *("cowshed") he looked like a skeleton. (83)*

There were, however, moments of hope. One Red Guard, Zhou Xiantong, was an assistant to Zeng who "risked his own life to preserve Zeng's scientific papers." The gesture and the risk involved must not have been lost on Zeng—some 30 years later, Zhou was still working as his assistant.

The intense pressure on academics began to fade by the end of the 1960s, and by the early 1970s, "the charges against [Zeng] were downgraded to 'historical problems'" (Neushel and Wang 84). Zeng and his institute went back to work. In 1975, as relations warmed between the United States and China after the events of the "ping-pong diplomacy" era, a delegation of Chinese scientists was arranged to visit the United States with Zeng as vice-chairman. There, on his first return visit to the United States in 28 years, Zeng met with President Gerald Ford, himself an alumnus of the University of Michigan.

Zeng Chengkui's life—from student activist, to ambitious and pragmatic scientist, to inmate starving in a cowshed, to foreign dignitary—rose and fell with the tides of politics in China. He helped shepherd an entire discipline and industry through the tumult, arriving eventually, as he described it, at oceanography's "elevation stage" (Zeng xiii).

Although the vagaries of political fortune affected them in different ways, all four graduates of the University of Michigan in this chapter were fiercely devoted to their country, whether that meant building up China's medical and educational infrastructure, researching new ways to feed her people, or guiding China into the nuclear age and international independence.

President Ford meets with the Scientific and Technological Association delegation from the People's Republic, 1975. Courtesy of Gerald R. Ford Library and Museum.

Zeng meets US president Gerald Ford, 1975. Courtesy of Gerald R. Ford Library and Museum.

Zeng and his wife (center) with colleagues from Scripps, 2000. Courtesy of Scripps Institution of Oceanography Photographs, University of California–San Diego.

Works Cited

Horsburgh, Nicola. *China and Global Nuclear Order: From Estrangement to Active Engagement*. 1st ed. Oxford: Oxford UP, 2015. Print.

Huang, Chia Ssu. "Medical Education in China." *American Journal of Surgery* 143.6 (1982): 660-663. Web. <http://www.sciencedirect.com/science/article/pii/0002961082900319>.

Huang, Chia-ssu, et al. "Surgery in New China." *Chinese Medical Journal* 79 (1959): 253-283. Print.

Lewis, John Wilson, and Litai Xue. *China Builds the Bomb*. Stanford, CA: Stanford UP, 1988. Print.

Neushul, Peter, and Zuoyue Wang. "Between the Devil and the Deep Sea: C. K. Zeng, Mariculture, and the Politics of Science in Modern China." *Isis* 91.1 (2000): 59-88. Print.

Ni, Ting. "Cultural Journey: Experiences of Chinese Students of the 1930s and the 1940s." Master's thesis, Indiana U, 1996. Print.

"An Open Letter and Zhu Guangya's Return Home." *Sohu.com*. 12 Feb. 2006. Web. <http://news.sohu.com/20060212/n241783744.shtml>.

Suttmeier, Richard. "The Academy of Medical Sciences." *Medicine and Public Health in the People's Republic of China*. Ed. Joseph Quinn. Bethesda, MD: Geographic Health Studies, 1973. Print.

Wan, Song, and Anthony Yim. "Jiasi Huang: 'A Surgeon and Something More.'" *Annals of Thoracic Surgery* 82.3 (September 2006): 1147-1151. Print.

Wang, Bing. "Wang Chengshu." *Biographical Dictionary of Chinese Women*. Ed. Lily Xiao Hong Lee. Armonk, NY: M. E. Sharpe, 1998. Print.

Zeng, Cheng-kui. Preface. *Oceanology of China Seas* by Di Zhou. Dordrecht: Kluwer Academic Publishers, 1994. Print.

Zhang, Shu Guang. "Between 'Paper' and 'Real Tigers': Mao's View of Nuclear Weapons." *Cold War Statesmen Confront the Bomb: Nuclear Diplomacy Since 1945*. Ed. John Gaddis, Philip Gordon, Ernest May, and Jonathan Rosenberg. Oxford: Oxford UP, 1999. Print.

8

The University of Michigan and Ping-Pong Diplomacy

By 1950, official relations between the United States and China had devolved to the point of armed conflict. As the two countries squared off on either side of the Korean War, ideological polarization infected both countries. For the United States, the Cold War meant a renewed fear of Communist power. In 1949, the same year the Chinese Communist Party (CCP) won their victory over the Guomindang Nationalists, Soviet Russia tested its first atomic bomb. Panic about Communist espionage and influence swept the States, and it wasn't long before a fervent demagogue, Senator Joseph McCarthy, led the country on an anti-Communist witch-hunt. Congressional bodies such as the House Un-American Activities Committee questioned and accused US citizens, often groundlessly, of having Communist sympathies. The new People's Republic of China (PRC), meanwhile, took a similar stance toward the capitalist West. During the political movements, power struggles, and internal revolutions that characterized the first two decades of the PRC, real or fabricated ties to America were often grounds for persecution.

The two nations split. The United States refused to acknowledge the PRC, prohibited US citizens from visiting, and instituted a trade embargo; the PRC worked to support Communist revolutions worldwide, creating ties with Cuba, North Korea, and North Vietnam. At the University of Michigan (U-M), the enrollment of students from mainland China dropped precipitously. As recently as 1940, China had sent more students to U-M than any country other than Canada. By 1954, that number had been cut in half, and a decade later, in 1965, the People's Republic wasn't even listed in the registrar's table of attendance from foreign countries.

But by the end of the 1960s, both countries had reason to hope for a renewed friendship. The Nixon administration in the United States, hounded by the increasingly deadly and unpopular Vietnam War, was desperate for some good news to give the American people. And Chairman Mao's CCP, shaken by the violence of the Cultural Revolution and by their dying alliance with Soviet Russia, began to seek a way to reach the United States. In the triangular power struggle between the United States, the USSR, and the PRC, a renewed alliance between America and China could provide both countries some much-needed stability.

And yet, after decades of official hostility, the United States and China both needed a face-saving excuse to reconnect. As it happened, they found their excuse in the unlikeliest place: the game of table tennis. And as usual, the University of Michigan managed to find itself in the center of the action.

Ping-Pong Takes Center Stage

The chance for rapprochement came in 1971, at the World Table Tennis Championships in Nagoya, Japan. The location made for less-than-neutral territory for the two nations—for two decades, the PRC had maintained a radio silence toward both the United States and Japan. But with some maneuvering, Zhou Enlai secured an invitation for the Chinese team from the Japanese table tennis organization.

The US and PRC teams couldn't have been more different. The US ping-pong team was a ragtag assortment of amateur enthusiasts—table tennis hadn't achieved the nationwide popularity in the States that it had in China. Instead, it was a basement pastime, a game hastily set up in seedy bars or recreation clubs. Tournaments, when they happened, didn't draw anywhere near the massive crowds that football, baseball, or basketball drew. The US team varied widely in age and experience, from 15-year-old Judy Bochenski to adult professionals working at IBM and the United Nations (Griffin 181): "The United States Table Tennis Association (USTTA) was still too poor to send a team, and the players were paying their own way"; Judy Bochenski's father had to borrow $900 from the bank for her airfare (180–181).

The official team from the People's Republic of China, on the other hand, was a finely honed instrument trained and sponsored by the government. For the Chinese team, sport and politics had long been intertwined. As early as Rong Guotan's victory at the 1959 World Championships in Germany, winning games had become a method of communication to both the outside world and Chinese citizens exhausted by decades of war and adjusting to the norms of a new ideology. The message to both internal and external parties was clear: New China was a strong nation capable of competing on an international stage; Maoist policies were working. Mao himself "called ping-pong China's new 'spiritual nuclear weapon'" (Griffin 85). As the Chinese ping-pong team began to win major victories, they became national celebrities, symbols of prosperity and vitality in years otherwise marked by privation. Association with top-level members of the CCP such as He Long and Zhou Enlai sheltered the team from the worst of the famine of the Great Leap Forward. And although their celebrity statuses had made them prime targets for persecution during the Cultural Revolution, by the time the World Championships in Nagoya came around, the Chinese team was still one of the most formidable ping-pong organizations in the world.

From a competitive standpoint, the United States had almost no chance of success in Nagoya: they were "ranked twenty-third in the world" and, according to Tim Boggan, vice president of the USTTA, "'there were no expectations'" (Griffin 181). Soon even the stars of the US team had dropped out of the major brackets, and many spent their time "sightseeing" (182). The Chinese team, however, had "scraped off the rust" accumulated after years of manual labor during the Cultural Revolution to take home the

Group photograph of the Chinese table tennis team in America, April 1972. Zhuang Zedong is pictured on the bottom row in the light-colored jacket. Bentley Historical Library, University of Michigan.

Swaythling Cup for their men's team; in the singles competition, star player and previous World Champion Zhuang Zedong withdrew from the tournament before facing a Cambodian player, saying that he would not "compete against 'players who represent governments [that are] enemies of the Cambodian and Vietnamese people . . . puppets of US imperialism'" (186–187).

While such a statement might have played well into the political climate at home in China, it did not bode well for the possibility of rapprochement. All it took, however, were two chance encounters to open a crack in the diplomatic door. Both encounters revolved around a young American named Glenn Cowan, a long-haired product of the counterculture movements that had shaped the 1960s in the United States.

Compared to the rest of the US and Chinese players, Cowan stood out as if draped in neon. He idolized Mick Jagger, wasn't shy about smoking pot, and had a natural instinct for both ping-pong and showmanship. In what would soon become internationally recognized as a kind of accidental, slacker diplomacy, during one practice session, Cowan waved over a young Chinese player, Liang Geliang, to practice together. "Liang thought of his invitation as 'almost an insult,' an American attempt to hoodwink him because he was so young. Liang retreated to ask an official what he should do" and in the end practiced with Cowan for a few rounds before bowing out (Griffin 187).

This whim invitation brought Cowan under Chinese scrutiny; he became "convinced that the Chinese were watching him." Some days later, Cowan left the gymnasium after practice and boarded the bus idling outside, presuming that it was one of the transport shuttles. Only once the doors had shut behind him did Cowan realize his mistake—he was facing the entirety of the Chinese team: "All agree that there followed minutes of silence, other than the mechanical roar of a large bus changing gears. Cowan was in a country where he couldn't even read a street sign with players representing a supposedly hostile nation" (Griffin 188). After several uncomfortable moments, Cowan broke the ice, speaking through the translator aboard the bus:

> *I know all this, my hat, my hair, my clothes look funny to you. But there are many, many people who look like me and who think like me. We, too, have known oppression in our country and are fighting against it. But just wait. Soon we will be in control because the people on top are getting more and more out of touch.* (188–189)

By all accounts, Cowan's presence and words caused some consternation on the bus—"the orders had been strict back in Beijing: Americans could be greeted politely, but they were the only country at the World Championships with whom the Chinese players shouldn't shake hands" (Griffin 189). Still, Zhuang Zedong, top player on the Chinese team, stood up at the back of the bus and approached Glenn Cowan. With one hand, he offered Cowan a gift, a landscape portrait of the Huangshan Mountains; with the other, he shook Cowan's hand. Reporters and cameras awaited the team as they stepped off the bus, and by the next day, photographs of the two smiling players made the rounds in international newspapers.

The visibly friendly exchange, followed by a return gift from Cowan a day later (a T-shirt emblazoned with a peace sign and the Beatles' lyrics "Let It Be"), sparked a furious round of behind-the-scenes diplomacy at the highest levels of government. Mao himself, 74 years old and seriously ill, issued the order to invite the American team to China. The order was relayed through Mao to the head of the Chinese delegation in Nagoya, who passed it on to the US delegate to the International Table Tennis Federation, who checked in with the US Embassy in Tokyo asking permission to accept the invitation: "'Just go,' came the immediate answer" (Griffin 197).

They went. The US team spent their week in China touring, sightseeing, and playing exhibition matches, all the while accompanied by some of the first American reporters allowed into the country in decades. They were welcomed with a mixture of hostility and hospitality. At one match, banners in the crowd carried mixed messages: "Welcome American Team," read one; "Down with the Yankee Oppressors and Their Running Dogs," read another (Griffin 217). Later, someone in a crowd threw a stone at some of the team members; meanwhile, they were invited to meet with Zhou Enlai himself, who spent part of the evening chatting with Glenn Cowan.

On their return to Hong Kong, the Americans were mobbed by members of the press hungry for interviews, and a poll in the United States revealed "for the first time ever, the number of Americans in favor of China's inclusion in the United Nations had vaulted to a positive majority" (Griffin 227).

Alexander Eckstein, the University of Michigan, and the Open Door of Diplomacy

The US team's friendly visit to the People's Republic was all the two countries needed to begin the process of rapprochement. A public statement from President Nixon expressing a desire to someday visit China led to his top foreign adviser, Henry Kissinger, making a secret trip behind the back of the secretary of state to meet with Zhou Enlai in Beijing. It was a momentous exchange, done when public opinion about renewed relations was mixed in both countries. The results of the trip soon became apparent: formal sanctions against China were eased, including trade and travel restrictions, and in the summer of 1971, Nixon himself appeared on television to announce that he would travel in person to meet with Mao Zedong the following year.

More than two decades of conflict and state silence between two nations were thawing at last. Soon the United States would vote to replace the Republic of China (Taiwan) in the UN with the People's Republic. All that was left to do was invite the Chinese ping-pong team to the United States for a reciprocal visit. For Graham Steenhoven, president of the USTTA, this invitation presented a practical as much as a political problem. He only had the week of the US team's visit to China to make the invitation, and given that the team's visit preceded Kissinger's and Nixon's, he couldn't rely on official support from the US government. Unlike the Chinese team, Steenhoven and the USTTA lacked funding. They hadn't even paid for their own team's travel expenses to Nagoya—how were they going to fund the entire Chinese team's travel, housing, and food costs for an extended tour of the United States?

This problem came to the attention of one Alexander Eckstein. Yugoslavian by birth, Eckstein had served as an intelligence officer during World War II before receiving his PhD from the University of California in 1952. Over the course of his career, Eckstein worked as a consultant to the US Department of State and taught at several universities, including Harvard. By the time he heard of Steenhoven's problem, Eckstein was teaching economics at the University of Michigan as a "China specialist"; he also happened to be the chairman of the National Committee on United States–China Relations (Eckstein, "Ping-Pong Diplomacy" 328). While members of Congress did sometimes call on the National Committee to deliver briefings or write memos, it was a civilian, nongovernmental organization.

This meant that the committee, unlike the US government, could help Steenhoven. Eckstein "immediately arranged a telephone conference with the officers of the National Committee, who unanimously agreed that the organization would find a way to raise all the needed funds and cosponsor a visit of the Chinese team to the United States." They set to work even before the US team's trip to China had concluded, raising funds, planning an itinerary, and contacting cities and universities that might be willing to host the Chinese team. Steenhoven made his formal invitation and received a favorable response from Zhou Enlai: "I believe that this new beginning of our friendship will win support from most people in both our countries" (Eckstein, "Ping-Pong Diplomacy" 328).

And then, silence from China. Eight months passed with no word as to when or if the Chinese team actually planned on coming. It wasn't until January 1972, as the groundwork was being laid for Nixon's visit, that word came from Zhou Enlai that the Chinese team would visit "when the flowers are in full bloom" (Eckstein, "Ping-Pong Diplomacy" 329). A less cryptic cable from the Chinese Table Tennis Association followed two months later—the team would be visiting on April 10.

The nine-city tour began in Michigan. The plane touched down at an airport in Ypsilanti, hometown of Gertrude Howe, who a century earlier had helped Kang Cheng and Shi Meiyu make their way to the University of Michigan for a medical education (see chapter 3). Awaiting its arrival was the entire US team, looking "positively shiny in their new uniforms . . . They looked like the crew of a cruise ship." As Zhuang Zedong disembarked, he reunited with Glenn Cowan; eager journalists snapped photos of the two men, arms raised, hands clasped, beaming with delight, and "the music . . . suddenly changed to a brassy version of 'She'll Be Coming 'round the Mountain When She Comes'" (Griffin 243). Alexander Eckstein and the National Committee were on hand to make a formal welcome. In his address, Eckstein wrote,

Portrait of Alexander Eckstein, professor of economics at the University of Michigan and expert on China policy. Bentley Historical Library, University of Michigan.

> *In welcoming you, we wish to express our appreciation for the warm and friendly hospitality you extended to our table tennis team last year and to Americans drawn from many walks of life since that historic turning point in the relations between the Chinese and American people. We hope that your stay in our country will be fruitful and enjoyable, and that it will be the first of many visits you will make to our land. (Eckstein, "Welcome" 1)*

Fruitful and enjoyable—by all accounts the visit was both, if intermittently. As with the US team's visit to China, the best-laid diplomatic plans were occasionally disrupted by cultural differences and activist interventions. The Chinese team bristled, for example, at a mistranslated sign prepared by a sixth-grader that mistakenly welcomed the "Republic of China" instead of the People's Republic; another cultural gaffe occurred on the team's first evening when, visiting the mayor of Detroit, the mayor waited to greet the team "at the first floor doorway" rather than walking out to meet them on the street (Eckstein, "Ping-Pong Diplomacy" 331). Such moments of tension were entirely accidental, but the Chinese delegation did face some deliberate resistance. During one exhibition match, a group of right-wing protesters dropped paper parachutes carrying dead mice on the audience, including one dressed in a red coat labeled "Kissinger"; others had pasted up posters that read, "Give us back our POWs" (Griffin 245) and "Keep your Ping Pong Players" (Eckstein, "Ping-Pong Diplomacy" 333).

Still, there were just as many moments of warmth. Ruth Eckstein, wife of Alexander, recalled that "the team's visit to Ann Arbor was very heartwarming. As the bus drove through campus, students recognized the Chinese, waved and cheered loudly." Out on the campus lawn, the Chinese team crossed paths with American students playing Frisbee. On impulse, they gave their disc to one of the Chinese players; compelled to give a return gift, he gave the only thing he had to hand: an orange from the University of Michigan cafeteria: "As the bus drove away, the Michigan undergraduate stood with the orange cupped in his hands, looking at it as if it were made of solid gold" (Eckstein, "Ping-Pong Diplomacy" 334).

As for the actual ping-pong, the theme long ago crafted by Zhou Enlai and repeated now by Zhuang Zedong was "Friendship first, competition second." A good thing too—despite their new uniforms, the American team was so outmatched by the Chinese that the disparity was evident even to the *Michigan Daily*, the student-run newspaper of the University of Michigan. "Gracious guests that they were," the *Daily* wrote, "[the Chinese team] carried their weaker American hosts in order to leave an air of competition to the proceedings."

The rest of the tour took the Chinese team to Colonial Williamsburg in Virginia, a re-creation of early life in America; to Washington, DC, where President Nixon echoed Zhou Enlai's hope that the sporting competition would lead to friendship between the two nations; and across the country to California and Disneyland, where "'they were greeted by Mickey Mouse, Donald Duck, Pluto and a six piece band' and got dizzy riding in swirling giant teacups. . . . A year before, real Russian warheads had been aimed at Beijing. How quickly life could change" (Griffin 253).

And by the end of the tour, it was clear that life between the two countries *had* changed. Nixon had become the first US president to visit China while in office. The United States had not blocked the PRC's appointment to the United Nations Security Council. And in 1979, President Carter would oversee the formal resumption of diplomatic relations between the United States and the People's Republic of China. As the Chinese ping-pong team's tour of the United States came to a close and the players parted ways at the airport, "genuine tears flowed on both sides. . . . They weren't the tears of indelible friendships but the recognition that something remarkable had happened" (Griffin 255). A pebble that began a landslide, the reverberations of ping-pong

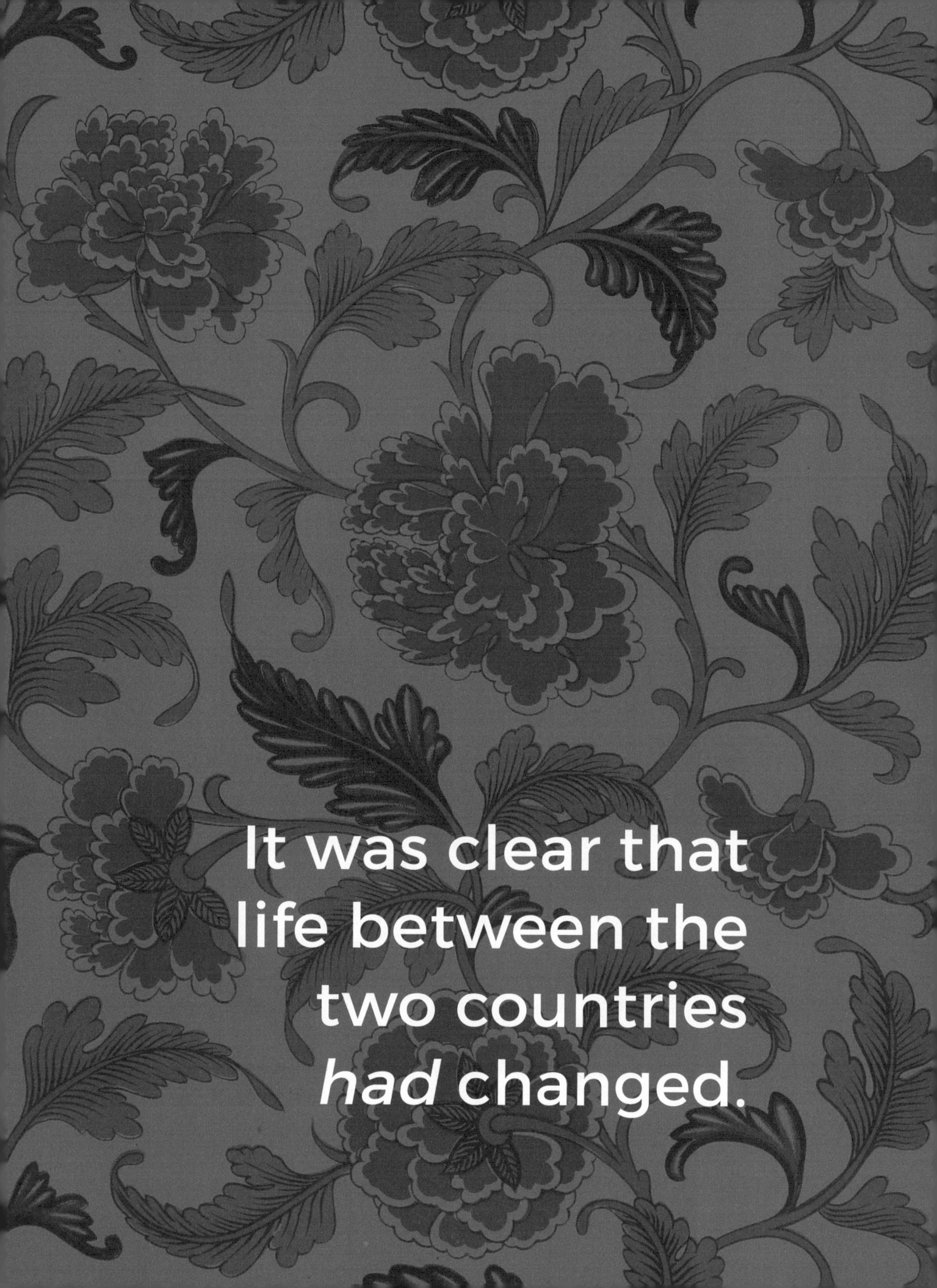

It was clear that life between the two countries *had* changed.

Donald Munro (second from left) in 1961 with his mentor Liu Yu-yun (second from right), whom they affectionately called "the Prince" for his relationship to the last emperor of the Qing dynasty. Photograph courtesy of Donald J. Munro.

A student in China photographed during the American Educator's delegation to China in 1973. Photograph courtesy of Donald J. Munro.

diplomacy shaped the geopolitical landscape for decades to come, altering the power dynamics of the Cold War and, in some small part, making room for a new era of reform in China.

Following Alexander Eckstein's successful efforts in orchestrating the final return volley of ping-pong diplomacy, the University of Michigan eagerly reengaged with China. In 1973, Eckstein's colleague and professor of Chinese philosophy Donald Munro co-led one of the earliest delegations of American educators to visit the People's Republic. By 1979–1980, although their numbers hadn't yet recovered the heights of the prewar years, the PRC was at least represented on the year's registrar report; the groundwork had been laid for what has become, in the 21st century, an inseparable partnership between the institution and the nation.

Works Cited

Eckstein, Alexander. "Welcome to the Chinese Table Tennis Team." 12 April 1972. Alexander Eckstein Papers, Bentley Historical Library, U of Michigan.

Eckstein, Ruth. "Ping-Pong Diplomacy: A View from behind the Scenes." *Journal of American-East Asian Relations* 2.3 (1993): 327–342. Print.

Griffin, Nicholas. *Ping-Pong Diplomacy: Ivor Montagu and the Astonishing Story behind the Game That Changed the World*. London: Simon & Schuster, 2014. Print.

Report of the Office of the Registrar. Ann Arbor: U of Michigan P, 1966. Print.

Report of the Office of the University Registrar. Ann Arbor: U of Michigan P, 1980. Print.

Report of the Registrar of the University. Ann Arbor: U of Michigan P, 1940. Print.

Report of the Registrar of the University. Ann Arbor: U of Michigan P, 1955. Print.

9 The University of Michigan and China

As of the winter semester of 2016, more than 40% of all international students at the University of Michigan (U-M) come from China, four times the enrollment of the next highest country. Clearly, the partnerships forged at the end of the 19th century and rekindled in the 1970s have roared to even greater heights in the 21st century. The work done by the individuals in the previous chapters to reach across cultural divides, to carve out new niches of authority and autonomy for underrepresented populations, to build new institutions, to jump-start whole disciplines—that work continues today at U-M.

Education Expands

More than a century after James Angell put his presidential duties on hold to serve as a diplomat in China, another University of Michigan president made the trip overseas. In 2005, President Mary Sue Coleman made a week-long trip to Beijing, Shanghai, and Hong Kong to strengthen the relationship between U-M and China. As Coleman put it, "Scholarship knows no borders . . . By our very nature, universities are at the forefront of globalization and cooperation" (Coleman).

China, meanwhile, was in the throes of a massive surge in demand for higher education. Just as the early 20th century saw the creation of some of China's most prestigious academic institutions, the 21st century arrived with a desire to make good on that intellectual legacy. In 2005, the year of Coleman's visit, the number of Chinese students enrolled in colleges and universities crossed the 15 million mark; just 10 years prior, that number had been only 3 million (Li and Yang 16). Coleman and the Chinese institutions she visited seized this historic moment to create a whole wave of new collaborations between the University of Michigan and China.

One such collaboration came at the request of China's Ministry of Education and National Academy of Education Administration, which worked with U-M to compose a Michigan–China University Leadership Forum. The forum, held in 2006, convened in Ann Arbor. Led by U-M faculty and staff and organized by U-M's Center for Research on Learning and Teaching (CRLT), the forum gave attendees a chance to share pedagogical and administrative strategies and to discuss "several major topics that the Chinese Ministry of Education . . . deemed helpful to the Chinese educational reform" (CRLT). Representatives from the highest levels of China's most elite academic institutions attended, and just a year later, a study conducted by members of the CRLT found that the forum had led to a "remarkably long and varied list of new initiatives." A primary takeaway from the first forum, it seemed, was an emphasis on "improving the student experience"; after more than a decade of explosive growth, the University leaders interviewed for the report indicated a desire to focus "on student services and student learning and . . . trying to instill new quality standards" (Cook and Zhu).

A group photo during the first Michigan–China University Leadership Forum in 2006. On the bottom row, left to right, are Edward Gramlich, then interim provost at U-M; Zhou Qifeng, then president of Jilin University and later president of Beijing University; University of Michigan President Mary Sue Coleman; and Wu Qidi, vice minister of the Ministry of Education, People's Republic of China (PRC). Photograph courtesy of Erping Zhu.

The first Michigan–China University Leadership Forum was enough of a success to continue biennially. The CRLT at U-M, America's first teaching center, became an international role model: "An eight-day Faculty Development Institute for leaders from 10 Chinese research universities" facilitated by the CRLT "resulted in the creation of 30 new model teaching centers by the Chinese Ministry of Education" (CRLT). As China works to implement a decade-long reform of higher education, the University of Michigan has been an eager partner, exchanging ideas and expertise with the leaders of China's academia.

A second major partnership began "as a simple research collaboration" almost 20 years ago (Redden). Dr. Jun Ni, a professor at U-M's College of Engineering, arranged to collaborate with researchers at his alma mater, Shanghai Jiao Tong University (SJTU). "'I thought maybe we could start some kind of partnership between the two universities to help them with curriculum development,'" Ni said in a 2014 interview, and soon his individual collaboration bloomed into an institutional exchange. In 2006, a year after Mary Sue Coleman's visit and the inaugural year of the Michigan–China University Leadership Forum, Ni's research collaboration became the UM-SJTU Joint Institute. "Guided by a board of directors made up of top leaders from both institutions," the institute offers a variety of engineering degrees with a "curriculum adapted from Michigan's" (Redden). The joint institute brings

The leadership of U-M and Shanghai Jiao Tong University at the signing ceremony to establish the joint institute in 2005. Photograph courtesy of Jun Ni.

international education home to China, with classes in English, dual degrees, and study abroad experiences available.

The joint institute (JI) has flourished since its early days, winning several national awards for model education and excellence in reform. In 2014, the joint institute "was the first Chinese institution to win the Andrew Heiskell Award for International Education." What's more, "since the first class of JI graduated in 2010, more than 80% of its graduates have continued on to pursue graduate degrees" ("Joint Institute"). The University of Michigan has been the happy recipient of many of these graduates, who have followed in the footsteps of scholars like Wu Dayou, He Yizhen, and Zhu Guangya, all of whom pursued graduate degrees at U-M.

The joint-institute model for collaboration between universities has been adopted by multiple other colleges within the University of Michigan. The social sciences division of the College of Literature, Science, and the Arts at U-M has developed a relationship with Fudan University, establishing a joint institute for gender studies at Fudan and funding collaborative research through U-M's Center for Chinese Studies. Grants of up to $10,000 a year for two years have been made available to encourage scholars from both universities to propose joint research projects. The institute has sponsored multiple international conferences, translated gender studies publications, and run several PhD credential programs and dissertation workshops.

An even more substantial partnership developed in 2010 between the University of Michigan Medical School (UMMS) and the Peking University Health Science Center (PUHSC). With a commitment of $7 million from each institution, they came together with the goal of enabling "scientists to translate basic research more quickly and efficiently into medical practice," ultimately improving patient health across the United States and China ("About Us," Joint Institute). And in the last seven years, the Joint Institute for Translational and Clinical Research formed by UMMS and PUHSC has already made significant strides. Since 2010, "the JI has funded 25 joint research projects involving more than 100,000 patients in both the US and China" ("May 2016"). In 2015, both institutions renewed their $7 million commitment, and there is every indication that the joint institute will continue its work for many years. It speaks to the urgency of the institute's mission that the challenges of joint leadership; of organizing research, symposia, and publications across the divides of culture, language, and distance; and of mobilizing two enormous institutions have all been overcome with such aplomb.

Cultural Exchange at the University of Michigan

Cross-cultural education has been valued at the University of Michigan since the early days, from Levi Barbour's scholarship endowment in 1917 to the educational

A group photograph of the Joint Institute for Translational and Clinical Research's Sixth Annual Symposium, held in the fall of 2016. Photograph courtesy of Amy Huang.

delegation to China led by Donald Munro in the 1970s. The year 2017 marks the centennial anniversary of the Barbour Scholarship, but it is not alone—today, U-M is full of avenues for cultural exchange.

Several colleges at the University of Michigan have developed unique study abroad programs for both American and Chinese students. The Gerald R. Ford School of Public Policy, for example, has created a course on US-China policy that culminates in a two-week-long trip through some of China's largest cities. The trip's organizer, Ann Lin, hopes that the epiphanies of travel will "upend [students'] preconceived notions about China" and that the program will "prompt students to return to China throughout their careers." In return, each fall, the Ford School invites "two professors from Renmin University in Beijing... to teach courses on Chinese economic and foreign policy" ("Renewing").

A similar exchange happens at the College of Engineering, where Dr. Lumin Wang, a professor of the Nuclear Engineering and Radiological Sciences (NERS) Department, began to organize trips abroad for University of Michigan students. "For a whole generation in the US, we weren't building reactors," Wang said in a 2016 interview. "Not only nuclear engineering students but also many faculty hadn't ever seen how a reactor is built." China, however, "has more than two dozen reactors ... under construction." For Wang and the College of Engineering, this presented a clear educational opportunity. In collaboration with Xiamen University, they created the Chinese Culture and Clean Energy Summer School, a six-week program at Xiamen University with an optional follow-up internship at the Shanghai Nuclear Energy Research and Design Institute. As with the Ford School, NERS offers a reciprocal exchange: "Shortly after the Clean Energy Summer School ended at Xiamen University, Professors Wang and Fleming hosted a group of 24 undergraduates from the university for two weeks in Ann Arbor," a stay that included lectures at U-M, field trips to Detroit, and a bus trip along the East Coast of the United States (Roth).

But as important as the study abroad exchanges can be, they represent the tip of the iceberg of China's presence at the University of Michigan. The Confucius Institute at U-M (CIUM), for example, is a bastion of Chinese arts and culture and "an integral component of former president Mary Sue Coleman's 'China Initiatives'" ("About CIUM"). Launched in 2009, the CIUM is just one of hundreds of similar Confucius Institutes scattered across the globe, each sponsored by Hanban, the Chinese National Office for Teaching Chinese as a Foreign Language, an affiliate of China's Ministry of Education:

> *Unique within the network, however, CIUM's focus is primarily on the promotion of Chinese arts and cultures, from the ancient to the modern, forming a strong arts component of former president Coleman's China Initiative, and advancing the university's global programs and initiatives overall. "The Confucius Institute at the University of Michigan will be singular among its peers, an extraordinary resource*

> *to all within the university community and far beyond," said Lester Monts, former Senior Vice Provost of Academic Affairs. ("Background")*

Under the leadership of James Holloway, Joseph Lam, Lester Monts, and Louis Yen, the CIUM has lived up to its promise. It runs cultural workshops for U-M students, including workshops on calligraphy and cooking Chinese cuisine; the institute hosts screenings of Chinese films at local Ann Arbor theaters, organizes lectures and symposia, and sponsors music and theater performances at U-M; and CIUM runs two separate programs, a Chinese studies program for U-M students and a visiting scholars program for Chinese faculty. And more programs are in the works, including a new student workshop about Chinese opera and theater and an online archive of all the Chinese art museums in North America.

The Confucius Institute at the University of Michigan has an academic counterpart in the University of Michigan's Lieberthal-Rogel Center for Chinese Studies (CCS). Named for Richard Rogel, an investor and benefactor whose vision for U-M includes a close relationship with China, and Kenneth Lieberthal, a professor emeritus of U-M and one of the United States' leading experts on Chinese policy, the CCS has a long history at the University of Michigan. While U-M formally inaugurated China Studies as early as 1930 with the Oriental Civilizations Program, the Center for Chinese Studies was formed several decades later, in 1961:

> *Rapidly it became a warm community in which the members' professional colleagues were also their social friends. It was an era of trans-disciplinary cooperation. Early on, under the leadership of Alexander Eckstein, a long lasting course on "China's Evolution Under Communism" was taught jointly by an economist (Alexander Eckstein), a political scientist (Alan Whiting, then Michael Oksenberg), and a philosopher (Donald Munro). In the same spirit, Professor of Modern Chinese Literature Yi-Tsi Feuerwerker*

A concert with Song dynasty chime bells organized by the Confucius Institute at U-M. Photograph courtesy of Jiyoung Lee.

A fashion show organized in 2013 by the Confucius Institute at the University of Michigan. Photograph courtesy of Jiyoung Lee.

designed "Arts and Letters of China," team-taught by her and by Richard Edwards (Chinese History of Art), and Donald Munro (Chinese Philosophy). (Munro)

Just as in the 1960s, the CCS "serves as a major intellectual hub for understanding China": for students at the University of Michigan, the CCS offers courses, interdisciplinary master's degree programs, and postdoctoral fellowships; for faculty, the CCS provides everything from travel and research grants to support for outreach and course development; and for the larger community, "many faculty associates have engaged in public service . . . as consultants to the State of Michigan, US State Department, World Bank, and even the White House," continuing the intellectual and diplomatic legacy of Alexander Eckstein ("About Us," Lieberthal-Rogel Center). Together with the Center for Japanese Studies and Nam Center for Korean Studies, the CCS belongs to the East Asia National Resource Center at U-M. To be marked a National Resource Center is a prestigious designation granted by the US government to a select few universities.

Taken together, the exchange programs, Confucius Institute, and the Center for Chinese Studies all show how far the University of Michigan has come since its early days in the 19th century. Where U-M once extended a tentative hand to China through missionaries and naturalists, we have now brought China home to Michigan, embedded in the heart of the University.

Toward the Future

The pace of the University of Michigan's collaborations with China is only accelerating, with more joint institutes, research partnerships, and student exchanges springing up every year.

The School of Natural Resources and Environment at U-M, for example, has created an accelerated master's degree program with the School of Environment at Tsinghua University, in which undergraduates from Tsinghua gain credits toward an MS at the University of Michigan. The School of Public Health recently signed a memorandum of understanding (MOU) with the West China School of Medicine of Sichuan

Albert Feuerwerker (right), history professor at U-M and founding director of the Center for Chinese Studies, with Fei Xiaotong, a sociologist, anthropologist, and social activist in China. Photograph courtesy of the Center for Chinese Studies.

University. Just as with the Shanghai Jiao Tong University Joint Institute, the initiative of an individual collaborator led to an institutional partnership. The efforts of U-M's Dr. Yi Li to help establish the West China Biostatics and Cost-Benefits Research Center snowballed into an MOU that "formalizes cooperation between the institutes through scholar exchanges, faculty training, collaboration in academic research and big data analyses, and establishing a joint institute" ("Cooperation").

The UMMS is at the center of two other recent partnerships. A joint program invites MD students from PUHSC to pursue a five-year PhD at UMMS before completing their medical degrees at PUHSC. "Five years is a long time," said Huilun Wang, one of the program's most recent students, "but I came for the PhD program because I wanted to explore medicine more broadly to find new treatments, new medicines for patients—something you cannot learn in just an MD program." With scholarship funding from Richard Rogel and leadership from Drs. Joseph Kolars, Eugene Chen, and Amy Huang, the joint program has been operating successfully for five years now, helping "develop a growing community of physician scientists" at PUHSC ("Joint").

Philanthropist Richard Rogel (right) with the recipients of his University of Michigan Health System-Peking University Health Science Center Joint Institute MD-PhD scholarship. Photograph courtesy of Wenying Liang.

A similar joint program under the leadership of Dr. Eugene Chen just graduated its first cohort of five students. Just "one part of a larger partnership, formalized in 2014, with Xiangya School of Medicine," this joint program invites MD students from Xiangya to complete a two-year research program at UMMS. Pei Li, a student who has already published work done through the program, explained the exchange's importance: "In China, most medical school graduates typically have two choices, to be a university professor or a practicing doctor," she said. "After this, I have another plan. I want to apply for a Ph.D. program and continue doing research" ("Medical School").

Today, the University of Michigan's partnerships in China extend even outside academia: "On January 19, 2017, S. Jack Hu, University of Michigan (U-M) Vice President for Research, signed an agreement with DiDi Chuxing, China's largest rider-hailing company, to develop scholarships and innovations related to the ride-share economy." A number of researchers from the Civil and Environmental Engineering Department at U-M will join the almost $1 million collaboration, a "joint research program" that will focus on "transportation optimization, big data, artificial language learning, and artificial intelligence" in the

A cohort of physician scientists from the Xiangya-UM joint degree program. Seated third and fourth from left are Drs. Eugene Chen and Joseph Kolars. Photograph courtesy of Craig McCool.

The leadership of U-M together with the Beijing Institute for Collaborative Innovation. Photograph courtesy of Chuanwu Xi.

For every step of China's growth and transformation in the last century and a half . . . the University of Michigan has walked right alongside China.

hopes of "better understanding transportation-behavior norms, reducing congestion on the global transportation infrastructure, and providing solutions to mobility" ("CEE Faculty").

And a new partnership with the Beijing Institute of Collaborative Innovation (BICI) will unlock the potential of University of Michigan researchers. A "system for collaborative innovation" founded by 14 of China's top universities, BICI provides technical support and funding for researchers trying to bring their projects to market ("BICI Fact Sheet"). Jack Hu helped bring U-M and BICI together, and now the partnership is under the guidance of Drs. Chuanwu Xi and Tiefei Dong at U-M. BICI "has agreed to fund U-M research and translational research in a broad range of areas, including engineering, health, science and environmental technologies from sponsored research" ("UM-BICI"). And in fact, BICI has already done so. In its first round of funding in 2016, BICI funded three projects in chemistry, biomedical engineering, and applied physics.

For every step of China's growth and transformation in the last century and a half—from the end of the Qing dynasty, to the turmoil of the era of warlordism through the war years, to the birth of the People's Republic, and finally to the rapprochement of the 1970s—the University of Michigan has walked right alongside China. The leaders and scholars who found the knowledge and expertise at Michigan to transform China set a high bar for those who have come after. The University has done its best to live up to the promise of individuals like Ding Maoying, John C. H. Wu, Zhu Guangya, and Wu Dayou. In the last several decades, U-M has thrown open its doors to the best Chinese universities, researchers, and students as if to old friends—*Welcome*, says the University. *Our best years are still ahead of us.*

Works Cited

"About CIUM." Confucius Institute at the U of Michigan, n.d. Web. 12 March 2017. <http://www.confucius.umich.edu/about-us/>.

"About Us." Joint Institute for Translational and Clinical Research. U of Michigan Health System and Peking U Health Science Center, n.d. Web. March 2017. <http://www.puuma.org/about-us>.

"About Us." Lieberthal-Rogel Center for Chinese Studies, n.d. Web. 15 March 2017. <https://www.ii.umich.edu/lrccs/about-us.html>.

"Background." Confucius Institute at the U of Michigan, n.d. Web. 15 March 2017. <http://www.confucius.umich.edu/about-us/background/>.

"BICI Fact Sheet." Beijing Institute of Collaborative Innovation, n.d. Web. 20 March 2017. <http://innovator.co/wp-content/uploads/2016/03/BICI-Fact-Sheet_EN_XZ_Final.pdf>.

"CEE Faculty Partner with Didi Chuxing for Transportation Research." *Civil and Environmental Engineering* 26 Jan. 2017. Web. <http://www.cee.umich.edu/cee-faculty-partner-didi-chuxing-transportation-research>.

Coleman, William. "Key Initiatives: International Education." *University Record*, 10 March 2014. Web. <https://www.record.umich.edu/articles/key-initiatives-international-education>.

Cook, Constance, and Erping Zhu. "2006 Michigan-China University Leadership Forum: Evaluation One Year Later." *Ministry of Education of the People's Republic of China*, May 2007. Web. <http://www.moe.gov.cn/publicfiles/business/htmlfiles/moe/s2994/201001/75811.html>.

"Cooperation between UM-SPH and WCSM/WCH." Ann Arbor: School of Public Health, U of Michigan, n.d. Web. 18 March 2017. <https://www.sph.umich.edu/>.

"CRLT's Work with the Chinese Ministry of Education (MOE) and Chinese Universities." Ann Arbor: Center for Research on Learning and Teaching, n.d. Web. <http://www.crlt.umich.edu/>.

"Joint Institute." Shanghai Jiao Tong U, n.d. Web. 28 March 2017. <http://en.sjtu.edu.cn/admission/joint-institute>.

"Joint PhD Program for Chinese Students Growing." *Global Reach*. U of Michigan Medical School, n.d. Web. 18 March 2017. <http://globalreach.med.umich.edu/articles/joint-phd-program-chinese-students-growing>.

Li, Mei, and Yang Rui. "Governance Reforms in Higher Education: A Study of China." *International Institute for Education Planning* (2014): n.p. Web. <http://unesdoc.unesco.org/images/0023/002318/231858e.pdf>.

"May 2016." *News and Events*. Joint Institute for Translational and Clinical Research, n.d. Web. 29 March 2017. <http://www.puuma.org/ji-news-events>.

"Medical School Helping to Train China's Next Generation of Physician-Scientists." *Featured News*. U of Michigan Medical School, 13 June 2016. Web. <https://medicine.umich.edu/medschool/news/medical-school-helping-train-china%E2%80%99s-next-generation-physician-scientists>.

Redden, Elizabeth. "A Look at U. of Michigan's Partnership with Shanghai Jiao Tong U." *Inside Higher Ed*, March 2014. Web. <https://www.insidehighered.com/news/2014/03/12/look-u-michigans-partnership-shanghai-jiao-tong-u>.

"Renewing and Strengthening the Ford School's Long-Term Ties to China." *Gerald R. Ford School of Public Policy*, 3 Dec. 2015. Web. <http://fordschool.umich.edu/news/2015/renewing-and-strengthening-long-term-ties-china>.

Roth, Kim. "Chinese Culture and Clean Energy Summer School: Student Exchanges Cross Borders and Expand Horizons." *Michigan Engineering*, 5 Oct. 2015. Web. <http://www.engin.umich.edu/college/about/news/stories/2016/october/coe-and-ners-students-visit-and-collaborate-in-china>.

"UM-BICI Partnership Program." *International Partnerships*. Research at U of Michigan, n.d. Web. 20 March 2017. <http://research.umich.edu/research-u-m/international-partnerships/u-m-bici-partnership-program>.

Links and Resources

Center for Chinese Studies at the University of Michigan
  <https://www.ii.umich.edu/lrccs/about-us.html>
Center for Research on Learning and Teaching, Leadership Forum
  <http://umich.edu/~crlteach/seminar/index.html>
Confucius Institute at the University of Michigan
  <http://www.confucius.umich.edu>
Department of Nuclear Engineering and Radiological Sciences, Student Exchange
  <http://www.engin.umich.edu/college/about/news/stories/2016/october/coe-and-ners-students-visit-and-collaborate-in-china>
Gerald R. Ford School of Public Policy
  <http://fordschool.umich.edu/news/2015/renewing-and-strengthening-long-term-ties-china>
Joint Institute for Translational and Clinical Research
  <http://www.puuma.org>
Shanghai Jiao Tong University, Joint Institute
  <http://en.sjtu.edu.cn/admission/joint-institute>
University of Michigan, Beijing Institute for Collaborative Innovation
  <http://research.umich.edu/research-u-m/international-partnerships/u-m-bici-partnership-program>
University of Michigan issue of *Chinese Chemical Letters*
  <http://www.sciencedirect.com/science/journal/10018417/26/4>

Design Image Attributions

Source: Jiao Bingzhen (焦秉貞), "New Visions at the Ch'ing Court," 1689–1726.
Source: Fan Kuan, "Travelers Among Mountains and Streams," c. 1000.
Source: Anonymous, "Suanpan in Ming Dynasty Novel," Ming dynasty.
Source: Zhi Chen, "Delight in the Winter," 13 November 2014.
Source: Zhi Chen, "Delight with the Red," 16 January 2015.
Source: Owen Jones, *Examples of Chinese Ornament Selected from Objects in the South Kensington Museum and Other Collections*, 1867, p. 179.
Source: Owen Jones, *Examples of Chinese Ornament Selected from Objects in the South Kensington Museum and Other Collections*, 1867, p. 49.
Source: Owen Jones, *Examples of Chinese Ornament Selected from Objects in the South Kensington Museum and Other Collections*, 1867, p. 141.

www.ingramcontent.com/pod-product-compliance
Lightning Source LLC
Chambersburg PA
CBHW042127100426
42812CB00017B/2644